THE
REINCARNATION
LIBRARY

MORNING FOR MR. PROTHERO

A Novel by JANE OLIVER

AEON PUBLISHING COMPANY
Mamaroneck · New York
2000

First Published 1951

©1951 by Jane Oliver
All rights reserved.

ISBN: 1-893766-18-7
Library of Congress Card Catalog Number: 99-80172

The Reincarnation Library™ takes great care in maintaining the authenticity, and therefore the integrity, of the author's original work. To this end, not one word of the original text has been altered. Please be aware that there may be phrases or characterizations in this book that the modern reader might find offensive. Such material is in no way reflective of the attitude of the publisher of this edition.

Æ, Aeon, Aeon Books and The Reincarnation Library are trademarks and service marks of
Aeon Publishing Company, LLC.

PRINTED AND BOUND IN
THE UNITED STATES
OF AMERICA.

For BET
who always believed
in Mr. Prothero

"I do not mean that the description which I have given of the soul and her mansions is exactly true—a man of sense ought hardly to say that. But I do say that in so much as the soul is shown to be immortal, he may venture to think, not improperly or unworthily, that something of the kind is true."

PLATO: *Phædo*. 114

"For spirits, I am so far from denying their existence, that I could easily believe that not onely whole Countries, but particular persons have their Tutelary and Guardian Angels. It is not a new opinion of the Church of Rome, but an old one of Pythagoras and Plato; there is no heresie in it . . . Even in this Material Fabrick the Spirits walk as freely exempt from the affections of time, place and motion, as beyond the extreamest circumference. Do but extract from the corpulency of bodies, or resolve things beyond their first matter, and you discover the habitations of Angels. . . ."

SIR THOMAS BROWNE: *Religio Medici*

"The wise man will follow a star, low and large and fierce in the heavens; but the nearer he comes to it the smaller it will grow, till he finds it the humble lantern over some little inn or stable. Not till we know the high things shall we know how lowly they are. Meanwhile, the modern superior transcendentalist will find the facts of eternity incredible because they are so solid; he will not recognize heaven because it is so like the earth."

G. K. CHESTERTON: *Blake*

MORNING
FOR
MR. PROTHERO

CHAPTER 1

"I want to get up," said Mr. Prothero, with all his remaining strength. "I want..."

"Tch, tch," said the nurse. She swooped over him, lifting him skillfully up the bed, and plumped out the pillows which had begun to feel like chunks of hot lead.

"They tell me," persisted Mr. Prothero, now scarcely above a whisper, "that they are calling on all the surgeons with experience. Apparently..."

"There, isn't that more comfortable?" The nurse pressed him relentlessly back against his pillows, smiling inexorably at him through horn-rimmed glasses. "Just you settle down for that nice little sleep we were talking about, eh?"

"Yes," whispered Mr. Prothero obediently. He closed his eyes, thankful for a number of things which at one time he would have taken for granted: for the temporary respite from the pain in his side, for the possibility of drawing the next few breaths without the exhausting struggle from which the sweat still lay in the deep furrows of his leaden face, for the diminishing creak and flutter which meant that the nurse was going to leave him in peace for a while. He had been ill, very ill. Sometimes he had wondered anxiously if it was all up with him this time.

It was not so much that he was afraid to die. But he'd always had a fancy to die in harness, confronting annihilation with the defiance of a man whose skill had been used to save so many lives that he scarcely grudged his failure to save his own. That would have been the way to go; on his feet, at his work, with the memory of all those he'd fought for to cheer his own going, with the familiar reek of antiseptics and ether still in his nostrils; the bubble of the sterilizer, the muted clash of steel in his ears, the high lights from the ranked instruments flicked up at him by deft movements, the brilliant arc lamp bathing the operating table in shadowless light.

But the failure of his eyesight had driven him from the battle while he had the strength of many victories still in him. Mr. Prothero did not curse God, but only because he did not believe in him. How could he? He had seen so much of human pain that surely the God who could permit it must be little short of diabolic. And the only alternative which appeared to him, the impotence of God to check the course of the universe he had created, seemed even worse. The thought of humanity, abandoned to its misery, had roused in him those tides of fierce energy which had carried him to the top of one of the greatest professions in the world, and yet left him with the simplicity of heart which made him sometimes long for the humble routine of a country doctor, as a gorgeous dignitary of the Church may sometimes think sadly of the opportunities of a parish priest.

For a country doctor, thought Mr. Prothero in the months of his retirement in the autumn of 1918, as he sat peering at the vaguely seen flames behind the bars, a country doctor lives in the midst of his people, sharing their lives as well as their maladies, loving and knowing them, watching and caring for them, glowing with their joys and downcast by their sorrows, sustained by their love for him when he comes to die. The remembrance of words heard long ago flitted through his mind: "Ye are members one of another...." But he pushed them away. They had a churchy ring. And he had no patience with churches or churchmen. Buttering their bread with fairy tales, the humbugging old hypocrites. No, he wanted nothing to do with them, either now or later. He'd done his work because he loved it, not because he was afraid of

God. He'd enjoyed his life, as long as they'd let him work. If he could work no longer he didn't care to live.

And this time he had undoubtedly been very ill. But he must be getting better now, or they would never have told him... just what had they told him? And who? The edges of their message were lost under the leaden tide of drugged sleep, but he liked to remember the clear voices which had held no doubt of his recovery as they spoke to him... on the telephone... through the habitual fog of his surroundings? Mr. Prothero could not be sure. Perhaps, he thought, with a little pang of apprehension, it had only been a dream. Wishful thinking like the nonsense the churchmen talked. But it couldn't have been, for the same voice was speaking by his bedside now. He knew it at once; it was young and strong, with a marked Scots accent. If it wasn't so much effort, he would have opened his eyes and looked the fellow in the face.

"We don't want to rush you, Mr. Prothero, but we're counting on you, ye see. In this emer..r..r..gency, we'll be wanting every-one we can get...."

"I'm a back number," whispered Mr. Prothero, so faintly that the words scarcely puffed out his white moustache. "Just a back number now, they tell me. You should round up the younger men..." he added with the slightest flicker of a rueful smile.

"It's your experience we're after. Tuts, no amount of theory's any good in emer.r.r.gencies," said the vigorous young voice

with its drum-roll of r's. *"You know that fine. It's you we want, Mr. Prothero. If ye'll come...."*

"If... I'll come?" said Mr. Prothero blissfully. "There's nothing I'd like more."

He would have tried to swing his legs out of bed at once, but caution restrained him. "Perhaps"—he felt conspiratorial as a boy—"perhaps I'd better wait till the nurse dozes off. Then I can give her the slip...."

"Right. We'll count on ye then...."

"Yes, you can count—" began Mr. Prothero. But he never finished the sentence, for his slight movement had brought on the dreaded breathlessness, and he was fighting again through the apparently endless vacancy of flare-stabbed obscurity that was so like the firework-spangled darkness outside the window of the London nursing home on that first Armistice night of 1918, through which persistent revelers still blundered and overladen taxis rocked.

But to Mr. Prothero the surge of noise from the street below seemed like the sound of waves breaking... waves breaking... breaking on a rocky shore, waves that he was trying for some unknown reason to resist in utter desperation. Then came a wave so great that he could no longer stand against it. The sea poured over his yielding body, overwhelming it in a strange peace.... He lay still with his eyes closed. Little by little, he almost dared to fancy that breathing was easier. His exhausted lungs no longer snatched each mouthful of air. He felt as if the waves which had battered him so cruelly were lifting him in newfound gentleness, were supporting him, bearing him along. Now he could hear other voices by his bedside, leaden voices without vitality.

"He's going, I'm afraid...." That was Ritchie, his colleague.

"Oh, obviously." He recognized the grudging voice of Adams, the heart man.

"Any time now."

"Any time now. Yes..."

"Pity. First-rate man in his time."

"Ye-es, I suppose so."

Mr. Prothero prepared to make the only comment rude enough for Ritchie and Adams. His throat still felt dry, cloyed with the metallic taste of morphia, but eventually he managed to gain control of his tongue sufficiently to say, concisely and very emphatically, just what he thought of them both.

"Tch, tch!" said somebody in a voice which was only pretending to be shocked. "I'm surprised at ye, Mr. Thomas!"

Mr. Prothero chuckled. He was enormously pleased. He had managed to make himself heard. But not, unfortunately, by Ritchie or Adams, it seemed. It had been a woman's voice. A woman... Mr. Prothero puzzled that out. He felt as if his mind were cushioned, engulfed, overwhelmed by cotton-woolly, billowing forgetfulness. A pleasant, but not at all an active, state. He must pull himself together, throw it off. After all, he had promised to get back to work again. This would never do.

Mr. Prothero tried to shake his ideas free from the surrounding vagueness as he might have tried to shake his head free from soapsuds. He had been ill. He had been ill enough for two of his distinguished colleagues to give him up. H'm, they'd been wrong there. That young Scots chap had thought differently. And quite right too. He was obviously getting better, Mr. Prothero told himself. He was too old a hand to miss even in himself the symptoms of returning strength.

"I feel..." he said slowly, astonished as he spoke, "I feel much...better."

But someone still loomed over him, and Mr. Prothero blinked as he tried to see her broad face more clearly. Its familiarity teased him with many memories, memories of wakeful nights, long ago, nights also troubled by fear and the strange forms of dreams, but comfortingly patterned by the jigging of tall bars against a cosy square of firelit ceiling overhead.

"You're doing fine. Ihmhm," she said. And her very voice filled his mind with blurred but kindly forms.

"Can I get up?"

"Tuts, yes," she nodded reassuringly. She bustled away and came back with his dressing gown and slippers. "You'll take no manner of harm from just sitting by the fireside."

"Very well," said Mr. Prothero. "I'll try."

He let her turn back the bedclothes and help him to swing out the long, thin legs that no longer seemed to belong to him in spite of the familiar pyjamas of faded blue silk. Then she showed him how to push his arms into the sleeves of the crimson dressing gown. Odd, how long it seemed since he had made these movements. And yet, so far, he was bound to admit that he felt no fatigue, no pain.

"I shouldn't like," said Mr. Prothero, still sitting on the edge of the bed, "to go through that last half-hour again. I don't believe death itself could be worse. Each breath . . ."

"Ihmhm . . ." she said soothingly. "It was vexing to see. But it's done with now. So what about that walk across to the big chair?"

To his astonishment Mr. Prothero found that he could walk.

Her arm was under his, and he was thankful for it, but his feet followed each other obediently across the carpet, falling with increasing firmness on each blowsy peony in the pattern, just as they had done when he was a schoolboy getting up for the first time after measles. Then, as now, he had walked triumphantly across the bedroom of Nanny's cottage, through the doorway and over the stone flags of the kitchen beyond. Then, as now, Nanny had been baking scones. They were still on the girdle that swung above the glowing peat. . . .

That had been in the Easter holidays, and he had been alone with Nanny in the cottage in the Scottish hills, with the rest of the family in London and the first daffodils opening in the orchard outside the kitchen window. It had been nice at the cottage. There was nobody to see what a fuss Nanny made of the big boy who needed her reassurance again, who liked to know she was there in the long nights when he was too uncomfortable to sleep, so that he called for drinks of water and she stayed beside him to tell the stories of the Western Isles that were backed by the comforting flicker of the firelight against the ceiling striped by the shadow of the tall guard, or grotesquely patterned by the silhouettes of vests and nightshirts hanging on it to air. They were wonderful stories, and Nanny's brisk, commanding voice always softened when she spoke of home. For Nanny was a Macdonald and her people had come from Skye.

Mr. Prothero's legs had folded abruptly beneath him into the old armchair, just as they had done on his first day up after measles. Then, as now, he had watched the girdle swinging over the peat. Then, as now, he had seen the steep lines of tawny hills slant up towards the tumultuous sky beyond the little window with its trim line of plants in pots. Then, as now... as now... as now... Mr. Prothero felt slightly dizzy. He shut his eyes and tried to get things straight....

For surely he had been taken ill in London? He remembered the first menacing grumble of traffic, the mounting roar of sound that announced the end of each age-long night. He had sometimes pictured himself escaping beyond it, out of his bondage, away from London, over the Border to the great hills that had meant so much to his youth. And now, here he was, in the cottage at Glaury Syke, looking out on a remoter horizon between the frilled leaves of potted geraniums. But he had scarcely seen Nanny's cottage for the past quarter of a century....

"I can't think what I'm doing here," he said.

The woman in the low chair opposite had picked up her knitting. The strong light from the window seemed to flash back from the needles in little points of brilliance that hurt his eyes.

"You'll always be able to find your way here," she said placidly, "while it's the dearest place ye know."

"Well, really," said Mr. Prothero. "Can you expect me to believe that my feelings have anything to do with where I am?"

"Have they not, then? Have they not, Mr. Thomas?" Nanny was smiling at him.

Mr. Prothero flung up an arm as if to ward off too great a shock. The elaborate fabric of the years that had given him so much, yet taken so much away, seemed to shimmer, to tremble, to collapse like the unsubstantial spinning of fine glass that was brittle enough to be shivered by laughter, and as it went the mist went from his eyes, so that he no longer saw the room about him as if it had been an underexposed photographic film, but clear and strong and sharp, receding into three dimensions, vivid with light and color. And beyond the black and scarlet rag rug that lay between them he could see Nanny's kind, brown, weather-beaten face, her little bright eyes the curious color of a peat-dark Scottish burn under a summer sky. The knitting needles no longer flashed, for she was holding both hands out to him as if she guessed that he would need their strength.

And Thomas Prothero, eminent surgeon and authority on several obscure complaints that distress the human body, was glad to lean forward and put his hands in hers. He was aware of an odd, tingling sensation at the base of his skull, which he noted, as he had been trained to notice all sensation, with interest, as a throw-back to the ancient, elemental response to fear that makes a beast's hackles rise and horror writers talk of a man's hair standing on end.

"What...what's happened?" His voice was shaken. He was inexplicably afraid.

"Why, lad, nothing in the world to scare ye," said Nanny in her steady, familiar voice. "Ye're here because when a body comes over the Border, he'll always find his way to the place that's nearest home."

CHAPTER 2

"Home?" said Mr. Prothero, aware of being comforted by the very sound of the word. "Home..."

He looked round the room, at the furniture he had known all his life, furniture that had come to Nanny from her parents; good, plain chairs and table and corner cupboard, sleek from a couple of centuries of strong-armed polishing by Scottish farmers' wives who made their own polishes as naturally as they made their own bread and cured their own bacon and dried their own herbs, so that all his happiest holiday memories were not laid up in lavender, but in a rich, composite odor, blended of farmyard dung and peat reek and new scones and golden beeswax and the home-cured hams that hung between bundles of dried mint from the hooks on the whitewashed ceiling, mixed with the piercing-sharp scent of burning grass and heather that drifted in from the hills where in springtime they burned off last year's old growth to free the growth to come. Mr. Prothero sniffed at it now, blissfully. Then he frowned.

"I don't understand..."

Nanny had taken up her knitting again; and he turned to look round the kitchen, recognizing with bewildered pleasure this piece of his past and that. Here was the cupboard in which so many things were kept, from medicines to candy-sticks. There was the table on which he had carved his initials with his first real clasp knife and been put over Nanny's knee and given six with the strap in consequence. That was the window he had broken with a cricket ball, the small square which he had afterwards been made to mend still clumsily puttied by inexpert fingers. There was the mantelpiece with its velvet cloth and fringe of crimson bobbles on which stood the honored photographs of his family. His parents were solemn and antiquated in Court dress, his elder sisters plump in frills and fringes or woodenly elegant in debutantes' trains and feathers, his brother Charles like a waxwork in the mess kit of the Brigade of Guards, and himself at thirteen, stubborn and freckled, clamped by an Eton collar, convulsively gripping his uncomplaining dog.

Technically, of course, his home had been with these people, in the big London house where his mother entertained continually because it was essential to his father's parliamentary career, and in and out of which he and his sisters drifted between periods of exile at expensive schools. And yet, he found he could recall scarcely one detail of the ornate mansion looking out over the wide spaces of Regent's Park. When they sang *Dulce Domum* at school, it had never been the image of the Regent's Park house which flashed across his mind. It had been the rough track leading up the Glaury Syke, the growing shape of the whitewashed cottage as he hurried towards it, picking out, detail by detail, the flanking outhouse and barn, midden and haystacks, the apple trees' crooked branches spreading in the angle of the sheltering walls.

"Home..." said Mr. Prothero again. But he added: "I still don't see how I got here."

Nanny's needles flickered at him. But she did not speak.

"I was ill in London," said Mr. Prothero with conviction. "So how in the world did I get up the Glaury Syke?"

Nanny finished a row and waved a needle noncommittally.

"Folks are often crossing the Border, and not keeping count of how they go," she said.

"But... I haven't been north for something like... dear me... for something like twenty-five years. At least..."

He broke off, his eyes wide, his jaw sagging a little. For, unless his memory were at fault again, the last time he had come north twenty-five years ago, was to a funeral... a funeral.... He stared in sudden consternation at Nanny's familiar, weather-beaten face, and the room seemed to haze, to rock slightly round him.

"I'm not feeling so well," said Mr. Prothero. "How did I get here...? I can't remember the journey at all...."

But Nanny, counting stitches, didn't seem to be paying much attention. Mr. Prothero spoke more loudly.

"D'you hear? I'm ill. Delirious. I'd better go back to bed. Such a journey... after an illness like mine. Who authorized it, I wonder? It might well have been too much for me in this weakened state...."

"Rubbish," Nanny said. "It's none so much of a journey, I'm telling ye, whether your ticket's single or return."

"Well, but the odd thing is," persisted Mr. Prothero, "that I can't remember a thing about it."

But Nanny made no comment. Instead, she started asking questions herself, her eyes amused, and bright as the clattering needles.

"Am I not telling ye," said Nanny, "that it's not enough of a journey for ye to remember it? Can ye remember every time just how ye rise of a morning?"

"Of course not."

"Or lay down to sleep?"

"How could I? Things like that," said Mr. Prothero, "that we do so often. Takes something unique, like death—"

"Unique?" She was laughing at him. "Use plainer words, Mr. Thomas, to a plain woman."

Mr. Prothero flapped a hand at her in protest. Words were formal things, like coin of the realm, in circulation among people used to similar coinage, carrying no meaning of themselves and useless for those outside one's intellectual boundaries. He sought for a means of exchange.

"Well," he tried, "we don't remember every time we sleep, because we sleep so often in a lifetime. I suppose death is memorable because it only happens to us once—"

"Does it now, Mr. Thomas?" said Nanny meekly. "Well, you're fine and full of book-learning. No doubt ye doctors have studied the question from all angles and proved the contention beyond any manner of uncertainty—"

"I wouldn't say," objected Mr. Prothero, as his habitual accuracy asserted itself, "that we've given the subject much attention. Our duty to our patients is to keep them alive, not to speculate on what—if anything—happens after their death."

He was aware of sounding pompous, more vaguely aware that this was due to distaste, even to fear. Disconcerted, he broke off in mid-sentence.

"Aye, just so," Nanny said. Her needles flickered at him with mocking agility. "Like bairns, we are, the lot of us, making bogies out of our own cleverness, if I take your meaning through your fine words, Mr. Thomas. I remember, when we were little, there was an archway near ma home that had been part of a great house lang since ruined. It led down to the seaside and we bairns ran in and out through it as long as the daylight lasted wi' never a thought o' fear. But scarce a one of us dared go that way in the dark for soon as the gloaming came down we remembered the old folks' tales an' screeched if the bigger laddies dragged us onywhere near it. The very same old archway it was, Mr. Thomas, that we'd been through more times than we could remember by daylight. That seemed just natural. Like sleep, mebbe, Mr. Thomas."

She threw him a quick glance over her knitting, then went on. "But in the dark, wi' fear all about us, from the whispered tales o' folk that knew no more than us, it seemed a terrible place, so terrible that none would go through it without they must. Like—death, mebbe, Mr. Thomas."

"The same gateway... the difference only in our own conception of it.... It might be so...." Mr. Prothero spoke as wonderingly as a child listening to marvels, but almost immediately the habit of a lifetime reasserted itself. His eyes, which had widened and darkened, as if ready to accept the evidence of things unseen, narrowed slightly, and he shook his head.

"We can know nothing at this stage," he said sharply. "And mere speculation, scientifically speaking, is useless.

Therefore it seems to me that we are bound to defer our conclusions till we are in a better position to implement them more fully."

"When ye were a wee boy," said Nanny to herself, "ye always talked most like a book when ye were the most uncertain. Ye've not changed, Mr. Thomas. Ye've no' changed at all."

Mr. Prothero found himself, unexpectedly, grinning like a schoolboy detected in a masquerade. "Uncertain? Of course I'm uncertain. On such a subject, how can anybody be anything else?"

"Just in one way, Mr. Thomas," said Nanny, measuring the sock she was knitting against the finished one. "In one way, that's all."

"And that is?"

"Why, by going through the archway in the dark, lad, and finding it the same for you as for them that run gladly through it in the honest light of day."

Mr. Prothero snapped his fingers, aware of being talked up a blind alley. "When I'm called on to make that journey, and if I by any chance survive it, I certainly shan't forget what you say. Meanwhile—well—it must be about time I went back to bed."

Nanny laid aside her knitting and rose. "That's as ye like, Mr. Thomas, but if ye'll just sit on for a wee while, I'll have your bed tidied afore ye get back in."

But when she had gone into the room beyond, where he could hear her plumping up pillows and smoothing sheets,

Mr. Prothero felt unexpectedly restless. Some of the things she had said, alien to his way of thought as they were, kept buzzing about him, unwelcome as blue-bottles, continually compelling his attention. However much he beat them off their importunity disturbed him still.

To distract his attention he cautiously stood up, steadying himself with a hand on the velvet-covered mantelpiece, and found himself looking at a photograph which he knew well, a rather ornately framed photograph of his son Andrew in his captain's khaki, taken early in 1915. Mr. Prothero's lips twisted with pain as he looked at it. He and Andrew had gone to have it taken on the boy's last leave before it happened. Andrew had come home after a long spell in the trenches and his delight at being back had made him so exuberant that even the solemn Court photographer had been obliged to join in their laughter. Even the photograph held Andrew's mood still, so that it seemed Andrew's very self who laughed at him from the formal frame, laughed so gloriously that his gaiety appeared eternal. Impossible to believe that that laughing boy was now in a Mental Home, his spirit quenched in the terrible blank docility of an idiot child whose vivid life had become as meaningless as a gramophone record with the needle stuck on a certain groove.

Odd that Nanny should have that photograph, thought Mr. Prothero. He'd had it in his study in the London flat. The frame had been Andrew's idea of a joke. Said it would last till he became a field marshal and needed something gaudier still. What a leave that had been. The boy had spent part of it in London because it seemed as if life could scarcely move fast enough for him after the deadly tedium of the trenches. But he had been down at Ringsey too, riding his pony Pepper at the local steeplechase, filling the house with friends, teasing his father and complimenting his mother and making up madcap parties for his sister Mary and Ted Gordon, the naval man who was later to marry her. Andrew's last leave...odd to contrast it with his own last visit, just before failing sight had compelled him to retire from practice, to the Home set apart for these young men with shell shock, so inexplicably maimed by the cruelty of war. He had still been hoping against hope, refusing to believe that the case was beyond any known cure.

Andrew had been brought in by an attendant whose unobtrusive presence had been apologized for by the superintendent. It seemed that Andrew's condition made him occasionally—unreliable. But Andrew had been perfectly, appallingly docile, as his father forced himself to go forward and shake hands with the blank-faced, rather plump young man whose movements were like those of a bewildered child walking in its sleep.

"Well, old chap, it's good to see you again. I've got lots of messages from the rest of the family. Your mother—"

"How do you do?" Andrew's voice had so little tone in it that it seemed scarcely human, and he formed the words with a sort of dreadful accuracy, his eyes not looking at his father, but roving round the room, while he held out his hand to be shaken as he had been taught to do.

Mr. Prothero felt the stream of small home news checked in his throat by such a wave of hopelessness that all his professional experience was borne down by it. But he struggled on, his hand still lying in Andrew's obedient, leaden palm, his other hand automatically patting his son's shoulder. Andrew was wearing the grey tweed jacket that his mother had sent him with his other things from home.

"Yes, you're looking pretty well, old chap. Getting on splendidly, I expect...."

"Thank you...."

Andrew's mouth was loose and vague, as if the will that controlled the muscles which should have expressed joy or grief, anger, interest or expectation, was no longer capable of being focused on the movements of the body which it should guide. Mr. Prothero, racked with pity, blundered on, pausing after each hopeful question in vain expectation of the slightest response.

"Your pony's been out at grass all summer. Remember Pepper and the steeplechase? We're having him brought in and got into shape. Mary's going to ride him this winter. She's settled down quite near us at Ringsey now. Remember her wedding? Her husband's in the Navy. Ted, you know. He's away, of course. But he bought the Cherry Orchard for her. Remember the Cherry Orchard? The Wards used to be there before they moved to the Old Mill...."

But the futility of it was obvious. Andrew's isolation was complete. He watched his father patiently, blankly, his brown eyes piteously anxious as those of a dog trying in vain to understand someone he knows to be friendly from the tone of his voice, but whose words are beyond his range of experience. Mr. Prothero trailed bravely on, naming this feature and that of the familiar past, watching for the slightest flicker of recognition, his voice faltering, recovering, rasping with the violence of his effort for self-control, trailing finally into silence.

"Thank you," said Andrew at last.

"Look here, old chap," said Mr. Prothero, "is there anything you want? Cigarettes—I brought along a few packets—"

Andrew's expression changed very slightly, and his hand made a vague movement towards the packets which Mr. Prothero was tossing on to the polished surface of the antique table which mirrored the flowers so beautifully arranged there by the superintendent's wife. It was as if the sight of the cigarettes which had been held in common among soldiers, to be the solace of crisis or boredom, had wakened the faintest echo of a fighting man's feeling for his friends.

"Matches, too," said Mr. Prothero.

"Thank you," Andrew said gently.

"Care for some magazines?" Mr. Prothero pointed to those lying on the table. But Andrew shook his head wearily. The sight of the magazines only recalled the terrible pains in his head which had followed his attempts to understand printed words.

"He's written a note to his mother, sir," said the unobtrusive attendant helpfully. "It's in his left-hand coat pocket. If you was to ask him—"

"Letter for your mother? That's splendid. Shall I take it to her, old chap? She'll be so pleased. Care to give me her letter, Andrew? It's in this pocket, isn't it?"

Mr. Prothero held out his hand, patting his own pocket in the way he had learned to do in order to help Andrew to reassociate actions with words. It seemed a very long time before Andrew understood and began to fumble clumsily in the pocket of his tweed coat. Eventually he produced a single sheet of ruled paper on which were several lines of large, perfectly formed, utterly characterless writing which looked like a page from the copybook of a child with an infinite capacity for taking pains. It was flawless and void, written to dictation in indelible pencil. Mr. Prothero looked at it for a long time before he realized that the officials were expecting some comment. Andrew was looking out of the window.

"I'm—er—delighted to have this, my boy," said Mr. Prothero. "I'll take the greatest care of it and see that it gets to your mother. Look..." He made a convincing little pantomime of the business of taking his wallet from his breast pocket, tucking Andrew's letter into it and putting the wallet back.

"See? Quite safe there, eh?"

"Thank you," said Andrew again. And then, as if he had become aware that something further were expected of him, he held out his hand, his lips laboriously forming his only other phrase. "Good-bye...."

The attendant took him away then, and Mr. Prothero found himself alone with the superintendent, a middle-aged man with an undistinguished face which contrived to be quite kind.

"I should like you to feel, Mr. Prothero," he said, "that everything, everything possible is being done for your son."

"Oh, yes," said Mr. Prothero. "Yes... of course. Everything, I'm sure."

"I think you wanted a word with the Medical Officer? He should be along any moment. If you'll just wait here, I'll go and see if he's been notified...."

The superintendent went ponderously out of the room, and Mr. Prothero sat there, waiting for a member of his own profession to tell him what he already knew. Andrew's essential life had been quenched, though his body lived on, might continue to live for fifty years. Never, in all his life, had he been so agonizingly aware of the tragedy of his calling, as when he sat there with Macbeth's challenge sounding in his ears, mourning the loss of his only son. For he might be one of the most celebrated surgeons in London, a man whose operations were considered models for a nation's students, yet neither he nor any living man, it seemed, could minister to this mind diseased; he could not pluck from even his own son's memory its rooted sorrow.

What *was* insanity, this terrible thing? What did it do? Andrew's fine body was untouched, he could walk and speak, see and eat, yet this substantial body was no longer Andrew, only in some strange way his ghost.

Mr. Prothero pushed the photograph back on the mantelpiece. Tears were streaming down his face so that he could no longer see where to put it down. Blindly he turned, anxious only to escape from his own pain.

"There, there, Mr. Thomas," said Nanny, at his elbow again. "Don't grieve so. He can still sleep."

"Sleep?" said Mr. Prothero. "I want him to live."

"So he will, Mr. Thomas. Did I not tell ye that sleep was an archway—"

"Fairy tales, fairy tales," said Mr. Prothero violently. "Leave me alone. My son—would be better dead—"

"Your bed's ready, Mr. Thomas. Come away," said Nanny peaceably. "Ye've done enough for now. Can ye manage by yourself, or will I take your arm?"

"I'll manage alone," said Mr. Prothero.

He shuffled across the kitchen, his slippers rasping over the flags, then muted by the carpet beyond. It was pleasant to slip back into the newly made bed, to relax against the skillfully piled pillows. Mr. Prothero closed his eyes, anxious to be left alone.

If only things were quiet he might be able to sleep, to find refuge in the oblivion about which Nanny had talked so much nonsense. Sleep, just nothingness, the short-circuiting of the brain by the action of the products of fatigue. Nothing more. Forgetfulness, escape. No, not escape, that brought him back to Nanny and her fairy tales. What use were fairy tales to a man whose life had crashed in ruin like a felled tree? Sleep was nothingness, nothingness, just nothingness. Whatever happened he must avoid the folly of wishful thinking. Sleep....

Why couldn't he sleep? It was still daylight outside. That might be it. Or all that noise in the kitchen. Nanny must have visitors, clumsy great oafs who were throwing heavy objects about the floor, clashing about in hobnailed boots, turning on the tap in the scullery, scrubbing and soaping themselves, and laughing. Laughing. Laughing. How could they laugh?

Mr. Prothero stirred restlessly on his pillows. Laughter was unimaginable. Nothing in the world could ever be worth laughing at again. Not with Andrew in that place, speaking like an automaton, holding out his soft, useless hand....

Then the bedroom door crashed open and a young man came in, whistling through his teeth and drying his hands on a rough towel. He was in khaki shirt sleeves and his hair was standing up on end, his face was tanned and lean and shining with soap, and he was grinning like a child out of school. Over his shoulder Mr. Prothero could see Nanny, beaming, with a mud-caked tunic over her arm.

"Hullo, Dad," Andrew said.

Mr. Prothero could not speak. His conception of the universe somersaulted into fragments and scattered into space with the violence of an exploding bomb. He just lay there, staring.

"Well, I do seem to have knocked you all of a heap," said Andrew cheerfully, rubbing his arms dry on Nanny's towel. "All right, all right. Don't look as if you'd seen a ghost. What's wrong with a bit of short leave? Didn't expect me, did you?"

"No...no...I didn't. I——" Breath came back to Mr. Prothero in little gasps, so that he spoke as if shocked by a sudden plunge into the sea. "I never thought——I'd no idea——"

"Neither had I," said Andrew. "But that's always the way. Got to take what's going when it comes to short leave. Gosh, I was glad of the chance of a clean-up when I got here. We've had three weeks in the line, you know, 'n' when I got the word I just put a few things together and jumped for it. Well, how's everybody this side?"

"I've——been ill," said Mr. Prothero.

"That's rotten. You're not looking too bad, though, now."

"I feel——I feel better," said Mr. Prothero. It was difficult to believe just how he felt. Better than he'd been for years...of course it must be just the sight of Andrew. It didn't do to count on such misleading flashes of strength. And yet——

"That's fine," said Andrew, tossing the damp towel down on the coverlet. "I've got all sorts of plans. Just you wait. I'll complete your cure all right. What you want is a day on the hills——"

"I don't really know that I should be up to much walking yet, old chap," said Mr. Prothero uncertainly. "I've been pretty bad, you know. Dash it, they gave me up—"

"Did they, indeed? Just shows they didn't know much about it—or you," said Andrew. "But you leave all the staff-work to me. If I can't wangle a broken-down old car to take us about the country it'll be a pretty funny thing. Do you all the good in the world, Dad—"

"I—I believe it would," said Mr. Prothero, in surprise.

Andrew picked up a comb from the top of the bow-fronted chest of drawers, where it lay with his father's silver-backed brushes on Nanny's crochet-work doilies, and began to slick down his damp hair in front of the small oval mirror on the wall.

"I always like this place," he said, tossing the comb down again and looking with appreciation round the bookshelves, the writing-desk in front of the small window, the immense prospect of hills which it framed. "Glad you landed up here too. That was a real piece of luck, if you like."

"You've been here before, Andrew?"

"You bet I have. So've you. Don't you remember?"

"Then—" Mr. Prothero wrinkled his forehead—"this isn't the first time we've met here?"

"Good heavens, no," said Andrew cheerfully.

Mr. Prothero put a hand to his singing head, overwhelmed by a rush of memory. One morning during the previous winter he'd wakened in his London bedroom with the fragments of a dream about Andrew still vividly in his mind, but jumbled together as the pieces of a kaleidoscope pattern are jumbled by a casual hand. He had lain there, trying to sort them out, but it had been too hard. Now, as Andrew spoke, the scattered fragments ran together into a memory so complete and exquisite that the tears came into his eyes. What was it Nanny had said? "Don't grieve...he can still sleep...."

"But—but that was just a dream," he said.

"Was it?" Andrew grinned at his reflection as he re-knotted his khaki tie in front of the little mirror. "Well, this trip's going to be real enough, Dad. You can take that from me."

And suddenly Mr. Prothero stopped trying to puzzle it all out. Tentatively, fearfully, he began to let himself enjoy this incomprehensible delight without anticipating its dissolution. He smiled back at Andrew's weather-beaten reflection. "As a matter of fact, I don't see what else I can do."

"Now that," said Andrew, swinging round on his heel, "is where you begin to talk sense."

CHAPTER 3

It seemed queer when Andrew had gone again. Mr. Prothero stood at the cottage door, watching him swing off along the track, burdened with his equipment, yet stepping strongly down the slope, the smoke from his cigarette hanging behind him, blueish on the quiet air. Beyond him the sun glimmered through mist above the western hills, so that Andrew's faint shadow fell far behind him up the rutted track. His heavy boots scuffed up the summer dust so that he seemed, from a distance, to be moving through knee-high clouds rather than walking on solid ground. When he had gone a few hundred yards he paused to wave, to light another cigarette, then set off again down the path. And then, almost in the blinking of an eye, the path was empty. His diminishing figure was no longer there.

Mr. Prothero peered into the distance, shading his eyes with a shaking hand, oddly disturbed by what must surely be a trick of the changing light. It seemed absurd that he could see Andrew no longer, that everything within a range of several hundred yards should be clearly visible... then nothing. It must be the mist coming down from the hills. Surely the obscurity was not due to his eyesight alone? The mist wraiths too were closing in, drifting to his very feet, blotting out the sun in clammy dampness. As he turned to go back into the cottage they swept before him, so that instinctively he put out his hands in search of the reassuring contact with the blistered paintwork of the well-worn door.

He stood there, gripping the door-posts, remembering how, as a small boy, he had pushed with an experimental finger at the big blisters of green paint that yielded so intriguingly to a gentle pressure as he flattened them with a finger-tip, then peeled off the soft paint with a finger-nail till Nanny's vigorous smack had put an end to that form of amusement. He looked down at the doorstep. It was decorated, just as it had always been, with the sweeping white whorls of Nanny's holystoning. From the kitchen came the steady rhythm of a table being scrubbed. Mr. Prothero let himself relax. Against the vast, winged incomprehensibilities of life and death such small, familiar things seemed to hold out friendly, comforting hands.

Outside the cottage door was a wooden seat, wedged between whitewashed wall and cobblestones with sturdy pegs. A smart, red-coated soldier had made these pegs, long ago. He'd said Nanny was too bonny for a widow woman and asked her to marry him instead. That had been down in the orchard, one summer's afternoon, when he himself, as a small, scared boy, had been up the very apple tree they were standing under, scarcely daring to breathe. She'd said yes, and the soldier had kissed her. But he'd never come back. And Nanny never spoke of him again. Mr. Prothero sat down on the seat now and closed his eyes. Peace beyond comprehension closed in upon him as he sat there in the evening sunshine. The small sounds of the valley and the hills blended in the quiet air as the dirling of the river encountered the tumbling cry of the curlew from the heights. This, thought Mr. Prothero, this is the truth... this is the innocent prayer of the creatures of the unspoiled world. This is something I knew once, something I had forgotten... something, perhaps, that Andrew... Andrew is beginning to learn....

Andrew... he checked himself sharply, and a chilly breath of wind shuddered across his upturned face. How could Andrew be both in the Mental Home and yet visiting Nanny's cottage at Glaury Syke? Unless Nanny's fantasies about sleep setting people free were true. Nonsense.

Andrew was mad. And yet, what was madness? Didn't we merely call everyone mad who no longer fitted into our scheme of things...our scheme of things...what reason had we for supposing that we knew?

"Mr. Thomas," called Nanny from the doorway, "will ye not come in to the fireside? It's none too warm with the sun near its setting, and I've infused the tea."

Obediently Mr. Prothero rose and followed her into the kitchen, where the recently scoured table was already dry and covered with a blue-bordered teacloth, and the kettle poured out a jet of steam from its hook above the fire.

"It's an odd thing," said Mr. Prothero as he went to his favorite place in the corner of the settle nearest the fire, "it's an odd thing, but ever since I've been here I can't remember seeing the sun rise. Every time I've given it a thought it's been over in the west above these hills."

"Ihmhm," said Nanny.

"Except when I was with Andrew," puzzled Mr. Prothero. "I remember noticing that it seemed higher in the sky then."

"Aye, so it would." Nanny did not look at him, as she went on pouring out the tea.

"But now it's evening again. It doesn't seem reasonable. You're not going to try and tell me—it can't possibly be because he's gone?" Mr. Prothero's voice was both alarmed and indignant, and he looked at Nanny as if challenging her to say anything of the sort.

But she merely nodded, lifting the teapot lid to see if more water were required.

"Nonsense!" said Mr. Prothero.

"It's no use your taking on so, Mr. Thomas. Time's different here."

"Here? Why here?" said Thomas Prothero, as if the possibility were a personal affront.

"Because we're over the Border, Mr. Thomas."

"Over the Border? What difference can that possibly make? Since when has Scotland had special clocks? It's absurd to expect me to believe—"

"Never you mind if it's hard for ye to believe it, Mr. Thomas," said Nanny soothingly. "Just take things slow. It's no' the place that makes the difference, but the state o' the folk. There's some that's in darkness at this very minute, and us in broad daylight, though the sun's near its setting."

"Well—of course—in Australia—"

Nanny shook her head. "I'm no' meaning Australia. No, nor any one country more than another. Nor is the Border I'm meaning just the line from the Solway to Berwick-on-Tweed, though it's as easy to cross for them that's willing. Mr. Andrew, now, has he not gone back, and never a question out of him?"

"Andrew thinks he's gone back to the Front," said Mr. Prothero slowly.

"Ihmhm," said Nanny, as she handed Mr. Prothero his cup of tea. "And what if he has?"

"But—" Mr. Prothero was troubled by an elusive, yet persistent memory. At last he grasped it. "That isn't possible. The War—the War's over. So—so where can Andrew have gone?"

"Back to the Front, Mr. Thomas, like he said."

"But—how?"

Nanny stirred her cup of strong, sugarless tea. "I'm not one of the clever folk, Mr. Thomas," she said eventually, "and there're an awful many things I'm working among that I don't rightly know the ways of. Time that goes round the clocks is just—just a manner o' speaking for the folk that like to set one thing afore anither. But the things ye pass by don't vanish when ye pass them. Does the road roll up behind your feet? No, it bides. An' time that ye call past bides on in the very identical way. It's back into the time he's passed by once afore that Mr. Andrew's gone now."

"Of course," said Mr. Prothero, "that's a known phenomenon in certain types of derangement, I agree."

Nanny sniffed. "Maybe aye. It's not for me to contradict them that's got book-learning. Mr. Andrew's mebbe taken refuge in the past, but he's no' gone back to a world of shadows. No, Mr. Thomas, he'll find the Flanders mud as real as the table that stands atween you and me. Aye, and real enough was the mud he brought. Did it not take me long enough to get it from his clothes?"

"Reality..." said Mr. Prothero in a bemused voice, speaking as if to himself, since he certainly never supposed that Nanny could answer him. "What—is reality? Does anybody, among all our conflicting theories, ever get a glimpse of it?"

"Folk are aye getting glimpses, Mr. Thomas," said Nanny unexpectedly.

"Yes, yes," said Mr. Prothero. "But I'm a surgeon. I demand more than vague hints and glimpses. I want proof."

"Mebbe ye do, Mr. Thomas," said Nanny soothingly. "But mebbe the glimpses are all our eyes can bear yet awhile. Will ye not take comfort in what other folk have found? It's all in the Book, Mr. Thomas, ye ken."

Mr. Prothero looked at her in silence, aware of the anger that always rose in him when a conversation seemed likely to turn towards religion.

"I—I am a surgeon," he said again. "I have seen men and women broken by pain and disease which—for which they could have no responsibility.... Out of every war, safeguard it as you may, there is a profit more hideous than the slaughter. It is—always it is—the innocent, trapped and maimed, who suffer. I have seen beauty blotted out, strength withered, my own son confined in a discreet asylum for those driven out of their minds. How can I love, how can I even believe in the existence of God as the maker and ruler of such a place as this world, whose sufferings must sicken any thinking man?"

"Here's a better cup of tea now, Mr. Thomas," Nanny said. "Yon last one was awful weak trash."

"You are the most exasperating woman," raged Mr. Prothero. "You've always been the same, ever since I used to come in to nursery tea in a temper and you'd just let me rail on till I was tired. Then you'd ask me if I wanted more milk. Don't you ever listen to what I say?"

Unconcernedly Nanny began to stack the tea things. "Oh, aye, I was listening," she said. "But many's the time I've heard ye on that question afore. It's always bothered ye. Nothing new there."

"New? Of course it's not new. That's what I mean. Century after century of human misery and desolation, and men struggling through their troubles so finely, so uncomplainingly that I—even I who am only one of them and not their Maker—am ashamed. If the will of God is human suffering then he must be a devil. If I—even I—would not willingly see one beast suffer for an hour, how can I worship a God who can contemplate the agonies of millions of helpless beings over millions of years?"

"Eh, wheesht, Mr. Thomas. Yon's wild talk." Nanny had picked up her knitting again, and the clitter-clash of needles made a small, homely sound after Mr. Prothero's angry voice had ceased. She said no more for a while, and he prowled restlessly up and down the little kitchen, mechanically stepping in the center of each flagstone as he had done when he was a small boy, though he had long forgotten the penalty he had made up for himself if he stepped on a line by mistake.

"I cannot tell ye the answer to that, Mr. Thomas," she said at last, "though I think them with learning would say that folk who were given free will were also given the choice how they would use it, and mebbe it's the wrong choice and not God ye must blame for the pains of the world. But there's one thing certain, if ye want the truth enough, beyond all other, ye'll find it at the far end o' the long road that ye follow home. But go canny, go canny, Mr. Thomas, in the search. For the truth's a terrible great thing, as far beyond man's imagining as the peaks yonder are beyond the peat-moss in the sykes. It's an ill thing to seek truth and forget love, Mr. Thomas. Go canny, now, go canny, for fear that ye're seeking more than ye can bear."

But Mr. Prothero scarcely heard her. He had stopped in front of the open door and was looking down the track that Andrew had followed, which showed up now, white in the gloaming. Above it brooded the familiar peaks, indigo against the pale sky from which the sun had set. The quiet of the cottage was as deep as that of one of the pools in the burn by which he had so often wandered, watching for trout, but against its profundity he fancied he could hear the clamor, like a waterfall, of voices that appealed to him out of the shadows of the persisting past, poignant with all the human pain which had embittered him against the incomprehensible silence of God.

"Doctor... it's bad again...."

"Please come. It's my wife...."

"Can't you operate? I don't know how to bear it...."

"I'm frightened...."

"He's dying...."

"Come at once...."

"Is there... nothing you can do?"

"Oh God... the pain again...."

"Come quickly... emergency operation...."

"I suppose there's no hope...?"

"It isn't right. Why should she suffer? What's she ever done...?"

"Oh God... help me...."

"She can't be going to... die? She's only three...."

"The pain...."

"The pain...."

"The pain...."

Mr. Prothero drew his hand across his eyes, restrained an impulse to put his fingers into his ears. Voices, so many voices, some shrill, some stoical, some scared, some sullen. He felt as if the whole burden of human suffering, bewilderment and grief had come down on his bowed shoulders, threatening to crush him beneath its intolerable weight. His body was ready to protest, to shrug off the overwhelming load. But within him something other than his body struggled to endure, to expiate, to understand, and to minister to the stricken world. He grappled with the terrible fact of suffering as with the unknown angel of Mount Peniel. His instinct urged him to hold on till he had wrested a promise or a blessing for humanity, though he knew not how.

"Teach me the truth," whispered Mr. Prothero, his face upturned to the pale and empty sky, from which, like a remote, incomprehensible reassurance the first stars now crept out.

In the kitchen behind him Nanny was lighting the oil lamp that stood on the plush tablecloth in the evenings after tea was done. Mr. Prothero could hear the glass chimney chime in her hands as she lifted it from the brass socket, the match purr as she struck it, could guess at the smoky flame that leapt from the wick, wound carefully down as she replaced the chimney and waited for the glass to warm. As he turned back into the room the condensation was clearing, and she had reached out to turn up the flame that picked up a slow sheen from tall press, corner cupboard and meal chest, gleaming from the graded pewter measures that hung above the settle and sleeked back from the black and white china dogs that flanked the family photographs on the mantelpiece. Mr. Prothero felt calmer.

"Sometimes," Nanny said, "I think that folks' characters are awful like this bit of knitting." She slipped out her needles as she spoke and began briskly to pull it down, winding the wool back on to the ball as it slipped easily from stitch to stitch.

"I don't know what you mean," said Mr. Prothero.

"There's a mistake in this," Nanny explained, "away back by the heel. And it's no use thinking that this sock's ever like to stand hard wear if I leave it the way it is. Yon dropped stitch mayn't show much, but it'll just start a hole the first time it's put on. I could darn it in, but I'd never make a perfect job that way. It's got to be taken down, real bonny work though it is, right back to where the flaw came. Now folks are often like that, to my way, Mr. Thomas. Ye think they're fine and wonderful, and ye're fair lost in admiration. But I'm thinking that sometimes the Lord knows where there's a flaw. It'll never show, mebbe, to them that's in this world, but it's going to make sore trouble for them in the world that's to come. Heaven's no place for flawed folk, Mr. Thomas. Mebbe that's why it takes us such an unconscionable time to get there."

"If we ever do," said Mr. Prothero wryly.

Nanny shook a needle at him. "That's a silly tone, Mr. Thomas, though I ken it's a queer great world for them that must needs understand. It's easier to be just an old body like me. For I cannot think that the Lord's like to be less particular wi' his creatures than I am wi' the knitting o' a sock. So I doubt we're aye liable to have to take ourselves back, Mr. Thomas, to the bit where we let a stitch go down. Aye, an' sorely provoking it must be, whiles, for them that seem to have got the farthest on and let a bit go, way back where it doesn't look conspicuous, mebbe, hoping it would never be seen."

"It's an interesting fancy," said Mr. Prothero wearily. He was watching her deft fingers, now quickly picking up the stitches and slipping them back on the needles, counting carefully to make sure that she had retrieved the missing one, nodding satisfaction as she prepared uncomplainingly to knit it all up again.

Jane Oliver

He went round the table and slumped down on the settle, elbows on knees and hands loosely clasped between. Nanny, in the rocking chair on the far side of the hearth, set it gently creaking to and fro with a rhythmic heel-and-toe action as her needles clattered round the diminished sock. Mr. Prothero was vaguely aware of being soothed by her presence, though without knowing why.

"I wish," he said, "that there was something I could do. They told me I was wanted. They told me I would be sent for. They promised I should work. But no call has come—"

"Maybe," said Nanny serenely, "they wanted you to get over the journey first."

"The journey?"

"Over the Border just," Nanny said.

"Oh yes... of course...." Mr. Prothero looked through the open door at the indigo peaks and the pale sky. "I suppose I must have come north somehow...."

"Tuts, don't let's start on yon silly talk again, for mercy's sake," said Nanny. "And you so much better for the rest you've had here."

"Yes," agreed Mr. Prothero. "I certainly am. It must be the air or something. Always used to set me up as a kid." He was aware of an eager, nervous strength, an impatience to try it on something new, and a capacity for experience which he had never thought to feel again. "I feel... fine," said Mr. Prothero.

From the rocking chair Nanny nodded and smiled.

"Of course it's ridiculous," said Mr. Prothero. "It must be merely a temporary improvement. How can it be more at my age? I'm an old man——"

"Ihmhm?" Nanny rocked more vigorously. She seemed amused.

"But I might as well make use of it while it lasts."

"Ye might indeed, Mr. Thomas. But there's many other things a man can do besides work when he's come through an illness like yours. Would ye not care to set out for the top o' the Peak like ye used to?"

"No, I should not," said Mr. Prothero.

"Or take a rod up the burn for a day wi' the trout? It's grand fishing weather."

"No," said Mr. Prothero.

"Then what about taking a gun on the moor?"

Mr. Prothero brought his open hands down on his knees in an emphatic gesture. "It's no use trying to tempt me. This may be the very place for a holiday but it isn't a holiday I want. I won't walk or fish or shoot. I've had enough idleness. You've got me well again and I'm duly grateful." Mr. Prothero smiled at her across the hearth. "You've been so good to me, just as you always were. But I don't want holidays. You know me."

"Aye, I know ye," Nanny said.

"And you know I'm bound to want my work."

"Is that truly so, Mr. Thomas? Do ye want it more than any other thing?" She questioned him gravely, her eyes vigilant over the tops of her glasses.

"More than any other thing on earth. I'd say more than anything in heaven if I believed in such a place," said Mr. Prothero. "You see, there's so much to do. They said so. They said I was to be ready. So——"

"Aye, aye, then ye want it badly enough. They'll be sending to seek ye any minute now, I'd think. If——"

"What's that you say?" Mr. Prothero's eyes followed hers as she looked towards the door, smiling at the young man who was just coming in. He seemed to be somewhere in the late twenties, snub-featured, sandy-haired, with the blue eyes and high cheekbones of the north. His profession was evident from the rubber tubing of a stethoscope which projected from one of the deep pockets of his shabby, leather-patched tweed coat. As he smiled at Nanny it seemed to Mr. Prothero that they knew each other well.

"Evening to ye, James," Nanny said. "Eh, he's been wearying for a sight of ye. He'll no content himself here."

"Hullo, Granny." He stooped to kiss her. "Good to see you again. Well, Mr. Prothero, I don't suppose you've the slightest idea who I am."

Mr. Prothero took the outstretched hand, noticing that the firm, cool pressure seemed to express so much vitality that contact with the strong fingers was almost like getting a mild electric shock. But what interested him most was the voice... the clear-cut vowels, the trill of r's... the associated memories of grey granite buildings—Edinburgh, the steep streets and the University. "No... I don't think I have," he admitted. "But surely we've spoken...on...on the telephone or something like that...."

"Aye, something like that," the young man agreed.

"I...I was very ill...." For a moment the memory of that struggle for breath swept over him, with a spasm of stress.

"Ihmhm."

"I thought I was done for." Mr. Prothero could laugh at the memory now. "Two of my colleagues had given me up, you know. Ritchie and Adams. Heard of them?"

"Oh yes...we know everybody in our line...."

"Well, what d'you think of that? Bit of a blunder, wasn't it? Of course they didn't expect me to hear. But I did. And it annoyed me, too. Never did think much of those two. Known Adams to make that sort of mistake before. Very fallible on diagnosis."

"Well, ye'll find we manage things better here," said the young doctor. "By the way, my name's Grant, James Grant. I've had instructions to contact ye, Mr. Prothero, as soon as ye've fairly got over the journey—"

"This blessed journey," Mr. Prothero said. "Everybody keeps harping on about it."

"It doesn't really matter in the least," said young Grant. "It isn't nearly as big a trip as people suppose. The main point is: are ye fit to start work?"

"I most certainly am," said Mr. Prothero. "Haven't felt as well as this for twenty years. I want to start work. I've got a lot of wasted time to make up for, you know."

"Mebbe it wasn't as wasted as ye think," said James Grant, running a hand through his thick, untidy hair in a typically abrupt gesture.

"You didn't have to live through it! Well, what happens next? Get me back on the job, Dr. Grant. That's all I ask of you."

"I'll do that, Mr. Prothero. If ye'll just come with me...."

CHAPTER 4

Mr. Prothero knew that the young man had taken his arm as they began to walk towards the door.

He was glad of that, for the kitchen had grown vague about him. Then things steadied down again. They were still walking, though their footsteps no longer sounded loudly on flagstones but softly on some sort of rubberized floor. They were not walking across Nanny's kitchen now, but along a lofty, cream-painted corridor, with great windows looking out on vivid gardens, and leading to a beautifully proportioned circular hall where doctors and nurses were passing to and fro beneath a central glass dome through which clear light streamed down.

"This is one of the largest hospitals in the reception area, Mr. Prothero," said James Grant. "Cases come to us for treatment from all over the world. Ye're going to be interested, I think. I doubt if ye'll ever have seen anything to touch it."

Mr. Prothero, who had visited at one time or another, most of the medical schools of Europe, did not quite like to admit the question which was teasing him. Presently he would be bound to realize where he was. After all, one corridor in a great hospital was very like another, though this one was actually pleasanter than most. Glimpses of gardens on either side suggested that the building lay in the depths of wide parkland. Ripening crops glowed in the sunlight which reflected distant gleams from a river which drifted between banks vivid with buttercups or pricked with iris spears. And beyond the river the land rose swiftly to a blue range of hills.

"A wonderful situation, I see," said Mr. Prothero. It reminded him of some of the newest experimental establishments in Vienna; there was a hint of a building he had seen near Stockholm, a suggestion of a celebrated institution he had visited in the United States. But this was nobler than anything he had known; it stirred him profoundly with its beauty, and its scope responded to his deepest intuitions of the destiny of man. "What a relief," he went on, "to see a place which does not seem to be hopelessly handicapped by lack of money."

"We have everything we can use here, I'm glad to say. But I know fine what it's like to be without." James Grant grinned ruefully. "As a wee lad my home was in a Scottish mining district. My parents went there from Skye."

Mr. Prothero nodded. He felt that he already knew this young man, whom he'd only just met, better than many other people with whom he'd worked for years.

"You got to Edinburgh?"

"I did that," said James Grant. "On a scholarship."

"One of the greatest medical schools in Europe."

"The very greatest, we'd have said."

Mr. Prothero chuckled. "I'm an Edinburgh man myself. Before your time, of course."

James Grant smiled. "Aye, mebbe. Well, here we are." They had reached the central hall, in which the architect had expressed the soul of his vision. It was very lofty, with the galleries of several floors running round it, yet so proportioned that the eye was not oppressed. It seemed to be built of some warm-colored stone which took on a high polish, yet gave an impression of lightness, almost of translucence, so that the rising galleries took the heart with them towards the central dome of clear glass which appeared to rest as softly as a soap bubble on the glowing walls.

"By Jove," said Mr. Prothero, almost in a whisper. "By Jove, what a lovely thing!"

It was some time before he could stop craning his neck and bring his attention back to the throng of men and women who came and went across the great open space.

The crowd, Mr. Prothero thought thankfully, was a familiar one. Just such a medley of people might be making their way across the hall of any of the hospitals he had known. Yet where, except sometimes in his infrequent dreams, had he ever seen so much color in a hospital before?

"We're taught here, ye see," James Grant was saying, "that all living colors have greater therapeutic properties than any manufactured ones."

"Yes, quite," said Mr. Prothero, rather absently. He was watching the people again, teased by the familiarity of certain faces. He shook his head and blinked. Inevitable that in any large crowd of medical people one could fancy stray resemblances to the great men of the past. Easy to think that grave professor had a look of a man whose name is commemorated in wards and clinics and the inconspicuous progress of innumerable lives set free from fear and disease. Easy, too easy, to let oneself imagine, in the odd, exalted state of mind that the place seemed to induce, that it was Lister himself who had gone gravely by, James Simpson who had paused for a moment to give directions to that slight nursing sister whose fine-drawn face was oddly like a familiar statue near Charing Cross. Just a fancy, of course. He must keep a check on himself. Evidently he was still in a highly nervous state.

"You know, I shall have to be pretty careful," he said aloud. "My brain's in a funny state. Just a moment or two ago I thought that chap over there was James Simpson."

James Grant grinned. "That's never a sign of derangement, Mr. Prothero."

"Of course, I'm only going by the portrait."

"Aye, of course," James Grant agreed.

"And that nursing sister—"

James Grant said placidly: "What I really want to show ye, Mr. Prothero, is the psycho-therapeutic department. It'll be most in your line now, I'm thinking. I know all about your surgical work, mind. But from what ye've been telling me about Andrew—"

Mr. Prothero looked at him sharply. When had he mentioned Andrew's name?

"I should like to see that," he agreed.

"We'll be getting along, then," said James Grant.

Mr. Prothero was surprised. "Are there no formalities? No registration?" he asked. "As a stranger, I should have expected to be asked for my credentials—"

James Grant smiled. "Ye're no stranger to us, Mr. Prothero."

"That's—er—most courteous of you," said Mr. Prothero. "But surely, if only to establish my identity, I ought to—"

"We don't have any formalities, Mr. Prothero. And ye were expected. People come because this is the work they want to do above every other thing. So we've no dead weight to carry."

"Indeed?" said Mr. Prothero.

"Ye see, there's no competition here," went on James Grant, as he led the way round an arc of the circle to an archway which seemed to lead to the psycho-therapeutic department. "No rivalry, no nice work between consultants, no funny stuff with fees...."

"Yet it doesn't seem to be pinched for lack of money," said Mr. Prothero as he looked round.

"It isn't," said James Grant with satisfaction. "We're given a free hand to build a system that's near as closely knit as if every available intelligence were working under a single control. What d'ye say to that, now, Mr. Prothero?"

But Mr. Prothero shook his head wearily. He'd heard this sort of stuff before. Dr. Grant was very young, very enthusiastic. Come to that, he'd talked in that Utopian way himself about fifty years ago, but he'd served his life-sentence in Harley Street since then. Men had their good points, but the best of them were mixed. They might have their interests, their knowledge, and their skill, but they also had their careers, their wives and their reputations to consider, their livings to earn, their spites and prejudices to indulge. No use trying to tell him that those things didn't count. He knew better.

"Come, come, Dr. Grant," he said briskly. "Are you trying to tell me that we've arrived in Heaven?"

James Grant chuckled. "No, Mr. Prothero, nor anywhere near it. We're still only on the way."

"H'm," said Mr. Prothero. "Even that may be in doubt. It's a longer journey, I fancy, than some people expect."

"And a shorter one, mebbe, than others dare believe," said James Grant gently. "Aye, but we aren't there yet, at all events. This is the same old world that you've trodden all your waking life, just seen from another angle, as ye whiles saw it in dreams. But will ye come now, and look at the place for yourself?"

They turned to walk down the wide corridor. At the first pair of swing doors Dr. Grant paused and they went into a long gallery.

"We're in the psycho-therapeutic department now," he said.

French windows opened from it on to a terrace, up and down which several elderly gentlemen in tweeds or flannels were pacing, some in pairs and one or two alone, their panama hats tipped towards their noses against the westering sun. Inside stood a number of bridge tables at which middle-aged men and women were engrossed. At the far end, in an angle of walls lined with portentous-looking books, various people rustled the pages of newspapers from the depths of armchairs. Through a doorway Mr. Prothero glimpsed a similar gallery in which younger people were playing table tennis or stepping through the French windows towards a swimming pool.

"These are first-stage patients," said James Grant. "They've just begun to come to us for short periods of treatment as and when they can."

"I take it," said Mr. Prothero in a low voice, "that none of them is—er—actually certifiable?"

"Tuts, no. And our clinic work is completely voluntary. It's one of the conditions of the Charter, ye see, that we may only treat people's mental state when they themselves want to change it. When they ask our help, they come here."

"Indeed?" said Mr. Prothero.

James Grant beckoned him towards one of the tables. "Come over here. They'll never notice ye. They still see only themselves."

"And how long do they stay?" Mr. Prothero was aware of the odd feeling of avid futility which seemed to hang over the card-players. "For hours, I mean, or days?"

"That depends," said James Grant, "how much they want to change. Some do no more than walk through. Others come regularly and stay till they're called away."

"Called away?" asked Mr. Prothero.

"By their ordinary routine," said Dr. Grant. "All these people are out-patients, ye see. Take this table, for instance...."

They paused beside a bridge table at which an emaciated woman with an elaborate tiara of white hair and an exquisitely made-up, haggard face, was dealing out cards. Her hands were loaded with bracelets and rings so that they clashed like those of a prisoner in chains.

"Mrs. Delamere," said James Grant in a slightly lower voice. "Now she's the much respected widow of one of the most eminent ex-Cabinet Ministers. But she's been a drug addict for years. Her capital has dwindled so that since her husband died she's barely been able to keep up her daughter's dress allowance. Yon rings are copies, ye understand. So there's been awful trouble, for the daughter was just running bills sky high. They'd taught her nothing else in the world at her expensive schools. But when there was next to nothing to pay them with, she thought herself terribly wrong-done-by, and little wonder. That was just the start, mind. She'd been engaged to a bonny young soldier, but the next thing was that he came back from France right out of his mind with shell-shock. So she broke it off. Aye, and within the year she'd married another man."

"Helen... Delamere," said Mr. Prothero in a stunned voice. "The girl Andrew was going to marry."

"That's so," said James Grant. "This is her mother. She was real vexed over yon marriage. She was fond of Andrew, ye see. She'd never a son herself. She took the blame for it, and the next thing was she began to come here. She started to give up drugs, too. She's still trying. Sometimes she gets on a wee bit. And sometimes she slips back. But she still comes here."

"Poor soul... I never knew," said Mr. Prothero.

"Yon man that's her partner, he's Mr. Holloway, the high-up Civil Servant. He's been a kleptomaniac for years. He felt he was losing his grip. So he started coming here. The other man is the head of a government department, but his private life's been a terrible series of shifts and frauds. They're beginning to get on his nerves. The other woman is a headmistress; eh, but she loved the power she had. She was a fair stalking terror. But since she's retired her mantle's kinda fallen from her. Sometimes she's scared."

"Why did they come, just those people?" wondered Mr. Prothero. "What's the difference between them and all the millions of successful, unpleasant people in any other part of the world?"

"Only the changing will," said Dr. Grant. He stood looking down at the bridge-players, who were as unaware of their presence as if they had been invisible. His wide mouth curled into an oddly compassionate smile, a smile which made the snub-nosed, shock-headed young man immediately remarkable. Mr. Prothero had seen that look before, on the faces of doctors, lovers and priests. It was a strange phenomenon, as if a light had been kindled somewhere behind their eyes. He changed the subject.

"It's an odd thing, you know," he said abruptly. "I keep thinking of it. I haven't seen the sun rise for dear knows how long. Ridiculous. It can't always be afternoon."

"Well," said Dr. Grant judicially. "That all depends—"

Mr. Prothero flushed with irritation. "Don't tell me it depends on the state of my mind. I've heard that one before. I'm not a mental patient. You'll be expecting me to believe that the sun's taken to standing still in heaven as they say it did for Joshua. Rubbish! I don't notice it, that's all. I'm suffering from intermittent loss of memory. My brain's playing me tricks. That's all. That's all, I tell you. It's enough. I can't remember when I last slept. I haven't had any food since I came here. Otherwise I'm perfectly normal. Perfectly normal—" His voice was getting shrill.

James Grant tucked a hand under his arm. "Steady," he said, "steady. It's all right. Ye're just catching a wee bit of yon people's anxiety. Shall we move on? The younger folk are in the next room."

Mr. Prothero followed him through the archway into another gallery. The ceiling was meshed with reflections of light from the sunlit swimming pool outside and the place was loud with the noise of gramophones. A piano was being strummed by a young man in uniform with a group of girls clustered round him. Balls clicked to and fro across the table-tennis net, several couples were dancing to one of the tunes in a small central space, others were sitting, confidentially, at small tables. A few girls were flipping over the pages of illustrated magazines, while other young men and women went in and out of the French windows, wearing bathing wraps or tennis clothes. Here, Mr. Prothero felt, the atmosphere was no longer leaden, but electric with discontent. Many of the young men's faces looked savage and frustrated, many of the girls pouted and frowned; but it was possible to believe that in all of them there was still a flicker of hope, a half realized desire to move on, to achieve more than a merely self-centered physical existence.

"Does Helen Delamere come here too?" Mr. Prothero asked.

James Grant shook his head. "When she was engaged to Andrew they often came over the Border. But since her marriage things have gone sorely wrong. So she never comes. She has to pretend too much, to content her pride."

"But surely—it was such a good match—"

"So she thought, poor bairn. But yon man's a sadist. She's surrounded with comforts, mebbe, but she goes in fear of her life."

"Good heavens," said Mr. Prothero. "Poor child..."

"Aye, poor child." James Grant was wry-mouthed. "We knew, of course, but she was set on managing on her own. So we couldn't interfere."

Mr. Prothero sighed, as he turned back to the jerking dancers. "Tell me, are these people getting any treatment? As far as I can make out they're merely duplicating their ordinary lives."

"That's all they can do at first. The thing is to get them here. Then just a wee bit at a time, as they come to want it, we suggest how things can be changed. Of course, mind ye, we lose a good many patients when the question of definite treatment comes up."

"One always does," said Mr. Prothero. "Well, what's next?"

Dr. Grant turned to the swing doors again and let Mr. Prothero out into the corridor. "Beyond the recreation rooms are the special clinics. Opposite them are the music rooms. They're always crowded with factory workers and people who have to work drills or drive underground trains. And these are our special consulting rooms."

He opened a door and Mr. Prothero looked into a pleasant room, informal as a man's own study at home. Two people were talking by an open fire. "One of our consultants," murmured James Grant, "and a patient who wants us to give him some really drastic treatment. He's from one of the bridge-tables. So ye see, they do move on."

"Yes," said Mr. Prothero rather vaguely. "Yes..."

"What's on your mind, Mr. Prothero?"

"My son," Mr. Prothero said simply. "I'm confused. You know, my memory's bad. I get dates mixed. Most old men do, I expect. But my case is more serious. I mix up things that happened ten years ago with things that only happened last week. Don't seem able to differentiate. Both appear equally real."

"Why not?" said James Grant cheerfully. But Mr. Prothero scarcely heard him. He was anxiously pursuing his elusive memories of Andrew.

"I thought," said Mr. Prothero, "that I spent some time with him quite recently, at my old nurse's cottage in Scotland, as a matter of fact. But of course I must have been confusing that meeting with an earlier one. Andrew—my son—has been in a mental home ever since he was sent back from France with shell-shock in 1917."

"Aye, mebbe," said James Grant. "But did my Granny not tell you that sleep and—well, sleep, anyway, could set most folk free?"

"She said something of the sort," admitted Mr. Prothero. "But really—"

"And she'd say that when folk crossed the Border they'd surely find the bit that was nearest home?"

"Home? Flanders mud—death and destruction—how could such horrors mean home to Andrew?"

"Maybe they would, if the lads he was with were dear enough to him, Mr. Prothero," said James Grant.

"I don't see..." objected Mr. Prothero.

"Aye, but ye will," said James Grant. "In a wee while, I'd like ye to have a talk with the director for a start. We'll just walk along to his room—"

Mr. Prothero was shocked by such lack of ceremony. "But I haven't an appointment. I don't know him. A man like that—he's probably booked up for weeks or has to say he is. See a stranger—at a moment's notice—why, he'll have to keep me waiting for at least—"

But James Grant grinned as he opened a door at the end of the corridor, saying: "Tuts, we don't go in for yon nonsense here."

CHAPTER 5

The director of the psycho-therapeutic department was a small, bearded man, with very bright eyes. His smile was quick and kind, and something about him reminded Mr. Prothero of the portrait of a certain Norwich doctor which hung in the library of the Royal College of Physicians in London.

He held out his hand. "Of course, Mr. Prothero, you've come about your son." His voice had none of the usual official detachment, none of the specialist's preoccupied haste. It was clear and warm and interested. There was,

Mr. Prothero felt, a certain reassuring simplicity about him and much good common sense. He went straight to the crux of the matter now.

"Well, he's just been admitted and he's doing very nicely indeed. You shall see him presently."

"Andrew?" Mr. Prothero was astounded. "Andrew—here?"

"Why not?" asked the director. "Many people come to us for short courses who are not ready to remain."

"But—" said Mr. Prothero, "I can't make it out. I spent some time with Andrew recently. He—he seemed perfectly fit. And yet—" He put a hand to his head. "I know he's really in that Mental Home. How can he be in two places, let alone three, at once?"

The director smiled. "He's just been sent to us for special treatment," he explained. "He won't be able to stay very long, of course. But at least before he has to go back we hope to have helped him considerably. He may be able to change over to a more normal life. It's difficult, at this stage, to make too many promises. But—"

"But has he left that place?"

"He thinks," explained the director patiently, "that he has come to us from the Front, and that he's in hospital with head wounds. Actually, of course, he got the earlier wounds when he first went to France, way back in 1915, and his recent injuries are due to an accident at the Home."

"An accident?" Mr. Prothero's voice was sharp with fear as he remembered that unobtrusive attendant.

Andrew, they had said, was sometimes—unreliable. But the director nodded confidently.

"An accident, Mr. Prothero. He fell from an upstairs window. One of the other patients gave him a clumsy push when he was looking out. He lost his balance and fell. The result was severe concussion, and he was removed to their hospital wing—"

"I suppose," said Mr. Prothero, "that this destroys any hope of a return to normality?" He had begun to pace about the room, ignoring the offered chair, on which the director now sat down himself.

"On the contrary," he said. "It actually offers the best chance he's had. You know as well as I do that shock's a queer thing."

Mr. Prothero turned at the far side of the room and came pacing back, his eyes on the carpet.

"We agree, I think," the director went steadily on, "that the being who has been shocked out of his right mind is probably reluctant to return to it because of a crisis which he is unable to face. But if a bridge between the past and the future can be constructed he may be induced to pass over it."

Mr. Prothero paused beside a chair, considered it, and finally sat down. "I should like to believe that, sir. I should like to believe it very much indeed."

"We shall ask you to watch it, Mr. Prothero," said the director. "We shall also ask for your co-operation. Do you remember the occasion in 1915 when Andrew was in a hospital in France?"

"Yes, of course," said Mr. Prothero. "A sniper got him soon after he went up to the front line. How d'you know about that? It was a purely routine case—one of thousands."

"Our records are pretty complete," said the director. "Well, the point is that Andrew has now gone back in thought to that base hospital. His memory of anything beyond the moment when that sniper got him has gone."

"But that's worse than ever—"

"It's a much better bridge-point, on the contrary," said the director. "He has lost all his fear with his memories. He is no longer retreating. He's ready to go forward again. He's longing to get well, to have another crack at the Jerries—"

"But the war's over," said Mr. Prothero.

"Never mind about that. It doesn't matter. He'll know you and he'll talk about his family and he'll want to get some home leave."

"My wife could never face it. We—er—don't see eye to eye about things. We've been separated for years, as a matter of fact. She never cared for my work. She's terrified of any abnormality—"

"I know. But your daughter isn't."

"Mary?" Mr. Prothero considered her. Mary was certainly a remarkable person. She had always, even as a child, had a quality of detachment, a sort of serenity, which insulated her from the rasp of minor irritations which seemed liable to undermine most people's characters. Now, with her husband at sea for months, sometimes for years at a time, without much money or help or companionship, she still moved through life as steadily as a candle-flame shielded by a strong hand. Mary, two years older than Andrew, and always, in the old days, his sure friend. "Yes, Mary could help him," he said.

"Good," said the director. "We'll ask you to get in touch with her presently. She'd take the suggestion more easily if it came from you."

"Yes, I think she might," Mr. Prothero agreed. "Of course, it's putting a big responsibility on her with Ted away so much. When I saw Andrew last—"

"Come and see him again," said the director.

They went up to the top floor, Mr. Prothero assumed, in a very fast lift. He had an impression of stepping into the corridor outside the director's room, where James Grant was waiting for them. But the sensation of emerging from the director's room on the ground floor and of emerging, presumably, from the lift into the glass-roofed corridor at the top of the building, were so blended that he seemed to have no memory of the intervening transit. Of course, his memory had taken to playing that sort of trick recently. But almost immediately he forgot his own problems in his astonishment, for the top floor of the psycho-therapeutic department gave him the unlikely impression of being inside a soap-bubble. Walls and ceiling seemed made of opalescent glass, and archways opened into wards which gave the impression of being hung with rainbows, varied by occasional glimpses of tree-tops and cornfields and horizon hills, admitted, as through tall windows, by panels of clear glass. There was light everywhere, brilliant but undazzling light which poured down on the sunburned, bandaged men in the vividly blanketed beds.

"They're all convalescents," the director said, "recovering from specially severe strain. There's your boy—"

Mr. Prothero went straight down the ward to Andrew, whose bed was at the far end. Andrew was already waving, and the other patients, reading or chatting, grinned in a friendly way as he went past. Mr. Prothero told himself that whatever happened he must behave as if everything was perfectly normal, as if Andrew had only been slightly wounded, hiding his own bewilderment as well as his delight, summoning every resource of the cool, scientific habit of mind.

"Glory be, I'm glad to see you, Dad," Andrew was saying. He had gripped his father's hand and was fairly pump-handling it up and down. "It's grand that you're here. I say, what d'you think of this place? Pretty wonderful, on the whole. Must be some old bloke's chateau or something. We're having the time of our lives...."

Andrew's head was lightly bandaged, and Mr. Prothero could see the yellow stain of iodine on the edge of the area of shaved hair. A scalp wound. Two or three stitches, perhaps. But, from Andrew's exuberance, it could scarcely be more.

"So they're doing you well here," said Mr. Prothero.

"They're doing us proud. It's marvelous. Never felt better in my life. Do sit down, Dad. There's a chair. Tell me the news. How's home? How's everybody?"

"Everybody's all right as far as I know," said Mr. Prothero cautiously. "I've been up in London, you see. So—"

"You work too hard, you know," said Andrew. "You ought to take it easy now and then. Heard from Mother, lately?"

"She doesn't write much, old boy. Never did, you know."

"No..." Andrew's face went blank, and for a few seconds his eyes were uneasy. He had known since childhood, in spite of carefully preserved appearances, that his father and mother did not get on together. Mr. Prothero went quickly on, before he could ask for Helen.

"You know that Mary's married?"

"Mary?" said Andrew. "Gosh, I don't believe it! She might have told me, I do think."

"You were—away," Mr. Prothero said hastily.

"Who's she married? If it's that chap in the Navy, it's all right. He's a good sort."

"Yes, it's Ted Gordon. You were expecting that, weren't you?" said Mr. Prothero non-committally. He himself did not care very much for Ted. A decent enough chap, of course. And yet...

"Hoping for it. I didn't know. At least..." Andrew rubbed his first finger up and down his nose in a perplexed way. "I can't quite remember. I seem to have heard something about it being all settled, now I come to think. It isn't a surprise—not really—"

"They've taken the Cherry Orchard, you know. Where—"

"Where the Wards used to be before they moved to the Old Mill?"

Andrew was interested, alert. There was nothing the matter with his brain, that was obvious. Only blank patches, perhaps, where things he'd known between the injuries had slipped out of their place in the pattern, so that now it must be put together again from the place where it had first gone wrong. Somebody had said something about that. Not one of the hospital people. Someone else, who hadn't seemed to have much to do with the remaking of lives. Only with things like... knitting. Nanny, of course. Nanny, pulling down a sock in which she'd made a small mistake.

"Yes, the Wards were there," Mr. Prothero said. "And Mary's got your pony, Pepper, with her. Remember Pepper?"

"You bet I do. Remember that toss I took at the steeplechase? Oh, gosh, I do want to see it all again. Have I been away for only six months, Dad? It seems like sixty years."

"Well, scarcely, old chap. It's a bit more than six months, though."

"How much more?"

"Tell him," said the director, as Mr. Prothero hesitated. "Don't worry. He can take it now."

Mr. Prothero said: "It's nearly four years."

Andrew put up a hand to his bandaged head, and his voice was incredulous. "Four years? Four—years? Glory, I must have copped a harder crack than I knew. Funny. It didn't seem much. It must have knocked me out pretty cold, though."

"It certainly did," said Mr. Prothero.

"But...but I must have missed the whole war," said Andrew, in consternation. "That's terrible. Me just lying here, I mean, all that time. I'm all right again, now. Can't I get up? Just to have a good crack at those Jerries. Just one?"

Mr. Prothero shook his head.

"You mean it's too late? Is it really all over? Now?"

"Yes, it's over, old chap. And I can't say I'm sorry."

Andrew turned and shouted down the ward. "D'you hear that, chaps? It's over!"

They grinned back at him, nodding, waving hands.

"You knew?"

"'Course we knew," said the man in the next bed. "You were out cold when they brought you along. Hadn't a chance to tell you a thing."

"Oh, well," Andrew said, "suppose I'd have tumbled to it eventually. Seems a poor show, though. Out of it all that time."

"Never you mind, chum. Thank your stars you can start in now."

"Something in that," Andrew said. Then his expression changed. "Well, what happens next?" He looked anxious. "Perhaps it'll be different. With Mary married and you in London all the time. Mother wouldn't like it if I didn't come home, and yet—it might be difficult. I don't know—"

"Would you like to stay with Mary for a while?" Mr. Prothero asked suddenly.

At first Andrew looked surprised. Then he nodded. "I certainly would," he said. "But—could I? Ted's a good chap. D'you think he'd mind if I came to stay for a bit?"

"He might be glad," Mr. Prothero suggested. "After all, he's making his career in the Navy. You'd be company for Mary when he was away—"

"Just for a bit," Andrew repeated. His voice was tentative. He looked scared. The news that the war was over had shaken him. It seemed as if he were now venturing warily across the bridge between past and present, half-guessing at the shadowy years which flowed below, carrying away so many things at which he had long been afraid to look. Mr. Prothero watched him in silence; it was almost as if Andrew were growing older as he watched. The noisy boy who had greeted him only a few minutes ago had gone and a grown man lay watching him out of the boy's candid eyes, a man who had left much of his irresponsible gaiety behind on the bridge from the past, and was now, very hesitantly, about to take his first steps into the untrodden future.

"It's going to be all right, you know," Mr. Prothero said.

"Think so, Dad? Think I could really go there?"

"I don't really see why not," said Mr. Prothero.

"Mary and I used to work things out," said Andrew. "It was all right when we were together, even at the Grange."

Mr. Prothero winced. He hadn't seen enough of his family. His wife had been preoccupied with her engagements: her charities and committees, her political interests and cultural luncheons. There had been no broken home. But there had been no unity, either. He saw now that Andrew and Mary had stood together against the desolation of that artificial structure, and the extent of their parents' failure was now indicated by Andrew's reluctance to return alone.

"Of course, now Mary's married I expect it's different—but perhaps you'd ask her, all the same."

"I'll ask her," promised Mr. Prothero.

"We could try and get through right away, Mr. Prothero," suggested the director. "Then we can get everything settled at once, and Andrew won't have long to wait. That's what you'd like, isn't it?"

"Yes, sir." Andrew's face changed as his grin flashed out. "Of course, I know it isn't really urgent or anything. I don't want to rush things. But—"

"But you'd like to know where you stand?"

"Exactly, sir."

"All right. Shall we go and see what we can do, Mr. Prothero?"

"Yes, of course. Well, Andrew, I expect it'll be all right."

"I expect it will, Dad." But Mr. Prothero was aware of Andrew's widened, speculative eyes watching them as they made their way down the ward, wading literally through the colors that shifted round them, warm as a summer sea. At the far end he turned back to wave encouragement. But Andrew's face had turned sideways on the pillow, and he seemed to have fallen, quite suddenly, asleep.

"Well, Mr. Prothero," said the director, as they went down the corridor, "shall we go straight back to my room and put that call through?"

"That's just what I should like," said Mr. Prothero.

"Good. Now, I rather feel..."

Mr. Prothero had just time to think that he didn't care for such extremely fast lifts, in which the very world seemed to drop from under him, before the director was offering him a chair in his study again. "Well," said Mr. Prothero. "Well...I must say I'd rather walk than use your lifts, you know. The speed...can't be safe...whew...."

"I'm sorry," the director said. "I'll see you're taken more slowly in future. But it's as much your own enthusiasm as anything, you know. You're so anxious to know about everything, aren't you? Can't bear to wait."

"Never could," admitted Mr. Prothero wryly.

The director smiled. "Well then, tell me about your daughter. Have you seen her lately?"

"No, not lately," said Mr. Prothero. "I've been in London. She was in the country. At the Cherry Orchard—"

"You know it well?" The director's voice had the quietly purposeful sound of a doctor talking to a patient just taking gas. But Mr. Prothero was already thinking of the Cherry Orchard. He scarcely heard him, though he answered dreamily, as if he were thinking aloud.

"Oh yes. I helped her to find it. It's an old Hampshire farmhouse, you know. Brick and tiles with a bloom on them, standing among fruit trees. I used to walk there to see her. It's quite near the Grange—my home—er—my country house. There's one room in particular at the Cherry Orchard...it runs the length of the southern wall...it has lattice windows looking over the rose-garden and a great brick fireplace with inglenooks where the gaffers could keep warm in the old days...Mary's favorite room. She's often there...."

It was at that point he realized that she was there now, in a blue dress with short sleeves, sitting at a table in front of one of the windows, chewing a pencil and making a face over an account book. She was moving the fingers of her left hand on the blotting-paper in a sort of five-finger exercise as she added the long column of figures, pausing anxiously here and there.

"...And five is fifty and six is fifty-six and nine is sixty-five. Put down five and carry six. That's easy for once. Hullo, darling. I didn't see you come in."

Mr. Prothero put his hand to his head in that little bemused gesture which had become a habit with him. "Didn't you, my dear? Well, I must have done, mustn't I?"

"Well, of course," said Mary cheerfully. "But you know what I am when I'm doing accounts. I'd scarcely notice the crack of doom."

"I haven't been very well," said Mr. Prothero.

"I know, darling," said Mary solicitously. "You were frightfully ill, to be accurate. I'm so thankful that's over."

"I don't think I'm quite right yet," said Mr. Prothero. "I'm not myself. My memory's bad. It plays me tricks."

"Does it, dear?" Mary looked at him out of the great blue eyes that were so serenely gentle. Her mouth turned down at the corners with understanding distress. "That must be sickening," she said. "But after all, you yourself are looking so amazingly better—you might be twenty years younger for the rest, you know—that surely a gap in the memory now and then doesn't matter very much? I mean, it isn't something that shows, and it doesn't hurt, like a broken leg."

Mr. Prothero chuckled. That was like Mary. Always so practical, though she had such dreamy ways. And there was something strong and sure about her, something that had nothing to do with what she said but seemed to be the result of all she was. He liked it that way. Mary might never say anything remarkable, and yet, there she was. Staunch as an oak, bless her heart. You were sure of her always.

"It's a funny thing, though," he said. "It's just over journeys. I don't seem able to remember getting about. I'm dashed if I can remember how I got here, for instance, how I came to be sitting here beside you in this chair watching you do your five-finger accounts just as you always do...."

Mary laughed. "That's easy enough, dear. The garden door's open and you just strolled in from the rose alley as usual, because it'd got a bit warm for your favorite seat at the far end."

"Perhaps I did," said Mr. Prothero doubtfully. "Yes, I seem to remember something about it. I stopped to tie up the rose over the porch...didn't I...?"

"I expect so. You always do. Every time you come in by the garden door. Or else it's the honeysuckle. I expect it's the rose this time. Look, you've pricked your finger."

Mr. Prothero looked thoughtfully down at the tiny gout of blood. "Well, I suppose I must really be here then, after all."

This time Mary really did burst out laughing. "Well, of course you're here, you obstinate old gentleman. Why not?"

"I thought..." said Mr. Prothero, in a vaguely troubled voice, "that I was somewhere else."

"Perhaps you were, love," said Mary. "Perhaps you've just had a lovely nap out there and only just come back from wherever you do go when you dream."

"D'you think people do—go anywhere?" asked Mr. Prothero in a speculative way. "Until lately I should have said that was even greater nonsense than most of the members of my profession consider it. Now... it's a funny thing... but I'm not quite so sure."

"Sure? Of course nobody can be really sure about anything," Mary agreed. "And I don't know much about what happens in dreams. I suppose it depends on where people really want to be. I can't bear to think of being anywhere else, so I expect I just stay here at the Cherry Orchard all the time, waking or sleeping, because I can't imagine where I'd sooner be." She drew a deep breath as she looked round the long, low room, with its cushioned window-seats, its latticed windows with their faded chintz curtains, its cavernous brick fireplace and butter-colored walls. "I'm so happy here I don't think I'd ask much more of heaven. Except, perhaps, that Ted could sometimes get a bit more leave. He's home again now, by the way. Did you know?"

"I didn't. Is he about?" Mr. Prothero looked vaguely round for traces of his son-in-law whom he scarcely knew and wasn't altogether sure he liked.

"No, he's in bed upstairs. He's worn out, poor darling. So I'm just letting him sleep on."

"Wise woman. Is he back from a long trip?"

"Pretty long. I haven't seen him since the Armistice. It seems ages. He's looking fine, apart from the fact that he's ready to eat everything in the larder and wants to sleep for a couple of weeks. He was on submarine patrol right through the War, you know. It must have been hideous, sometimes, especially knowing just how bad things were in the worst days."

Mr. Prothero nodded. "Oh, by the way, I've remembered what I came along to tell you. It's about Andrew. I've been in touch with the people in charge of him and they surprised me by being more helpful than I'd ever dared to expect. You knew about that fall he had recently?"

She nodded. "Yes, of course. He's been unconscious for days. They said anything might happen. I gathered they were completely in the dark. We've been told to be ready for news at any time. Of course they said it was almost bound to be bad news, because that's the way their minds work. But they didn't actually close the door to any hope of improvement when I tackled them about it. Such a thing had actually even been known to put the original damage right. Have you seen Andrew himself?"

"I have," said Mr. Prothero.

"And—has he come round?"

"He certainly has." Mr. Prothero beamed, and Mary held out both hands.

"Daddy, how absolutely marvelous. You've spoken to him? Was he quite sensible? What did he say? Do tell me quickly. I'm so absolutely thrilled. Andrew and I were such extra special pals in the old days. I can't say what it's been like to know he was—away. Do go on, darling. Why won't you tell me?"

"For the very simple reason that I can't get in a word," said Mr. Prothero amiably. "Tell you? Isn't that just the very thing I came to do?"

"I won't say another thing," said Mary. She put her clenched fist to her mouth and waited for him with widening eyes. Mr. Prothero patted her other hand and began.

"Well, to cut a long story much shorter than I feel inclined to do, I saw Andrew, fully conscious and entirely in his right mind. As you know, I'd never dared to hope for that—"

"I had, I had," Mary said.

"Well, it seems you were right. They were very pleased with him. They said—" Mr. Prothero frowned as he tried to recall the director's words—"they said that this offered the best chance yet."

"That's perfectly wonderful," Mary said. "Well now, what does Andrew want us to do?"

"What Andrew wants," said Mr. Prothero, "is to get out of that place just as soon as he can."

"And will they let him?"

"I think so. They seemed perfectly willing to agree, as far as I could make out."

"I suppose he'll go home to the Grange," said Mary, rather sadly. "To Mother." She looked so disappointed that Mr. Prothero went quickly on.

"That isn't his idea at all, as a matter of fact. What he wants is—Mary, do you think you would have him here for a while? What would Ted say? I know it's sudden—"

"Sudden? Of course it's sudden," said Mary delightedly. "The big things always are. And most certainly he can come. Ted thinks the world of him. And you know already that there's nothing I'd like more. Poor darling, he must feel so lost, so... so newly born."

"I think that's just about how he does feel," said Mr. Prothero. "You see, Mary, it's really rather difficult. You remember the head injury he got in 1915, just after he went out to France?"

"I should think I do," Mary said.

"Well, it seems that this second head injury has jolted him back to the time when he got the first. All the time between the Passchendaele campaign and the Armistice, everything till the moment he woke up in the hospital again has gone right out. They said it was as if he'd bridged the time between past and present."

"I can see that," Mary said.

"So that he passed right over the scenes which shocked him so badly that he couldn't face life at all."

"Yes, I know," Mary said. "There used to be a game we played when we were kids. It was called The Prince's Quest, and it had a great board with numbered journeys that led home through all sorts of terrible adventures like enchanted woods and fiery lakes and witches' caverns. If you threw the right number you might get carried over the sea of darkness, but if you threw wrong you had to count backwards till you came to something that broke the spell."

"I gather this is psychologically something of that kind," said Mr. Prothero. "By the way, there was one thing that made me wonder if Andrew really was going to be all right. Just something that I was expecting to be asked about if he'd really been himself. And since he never asked, I began to worry—"

"What was that?"

"He never asked me about Helen," Mr. Prothero said. "Now surely—you know how he adored that girl—wouldn't she be the first person he'd want to hear about?"

Mary bit her lip. Then her face cleared. "But, darling, doesn't Andrew's bridge go from early in 1915?"

Mr. Prothero nodded.

"He didn't meet Helen till the end of the year."

"Of course." Mr. Prothero brought his palms down on his knees in his favorite emphatic gesture. "Thank heaven for that. In the circumstances, that's going to make things a very great deal simpler, isn't it?"

"It certainly is," Mary said with a wry smile.

"Well now, about having Andrew here. You think it's quite a good idea?"

"I think it's the only idea anybody could possibly have," said Mary emphatically. "Hullo, what was that?"

"I didn't hear anything."

"It was Ted calling for me, I think," said Mary, spilling the cat off her knee as she rose. "I'd better go and see if he wants something to eat."

"And I think," said Mr. Prothero, as the odd, sinking sensation of strangeness came gently over him, "that perhaps I ought to be getting back, too."

"All right, darling. Come again soon," said Mary over her shoulder.

"I certainly will," said Mr. Prothero, turning in his chair to smile after her. But he found himself looking instead at a small, kind man with a brown beard.

CHAPTER 6

Mary Gordon sat opposite her husband at the gate-legged breakfast table in the long room at the Cherry Orchard. He reached for his fourth piece of toast and smiled contentedly at her.

"More coffee, darling?"

"Please."

She handed him the butter and took his cup. The toast crackled pleasantly as he spread it, and the smell of coffee and roses and haymaking made Ted feel so good that he wanted to say something about it. But he hadn't the words. Some years ago a schoolmaster had written of him: "Not a verbal type," and it was still true. It didn't mean that he didn't enjoy things. He certainly did. To be home, sitting there casually in sports shirt and flannel trousers, able to stretch his legs below his own breakfast table; to have a wife like Mary; to know that young Michael was in his cot upstairs in the nursery; it was a pity he couldn't tell Mary just how he felt about it all. But she knew. And she could talk for all three of them, bless her quick tongue.

Mary filled his coffee cup for the third time and then refilled her own. And then she sat thoughtfully stirring her coffee and staring at the great bowl of roses that Ted had been enjoying so much. Her expression was so odd that Ted eventually noticed it.

"What's up, love?"

Mary looked blank for a moment. Then she smiled again. "I just wanted to remember," she said. "And the roses reminded me. I had the most vivid dream about Daddy last night. He was here—"

"Ihmhm?" said Ted, reaching for the marmalade.

"Here in this room, talking to me, just as he used to talk before he was ill."

"Funny things, dreams," said Ted, taking a mouthful of coffee, then making a grimace. "Ugh, no sugar at all."

"Sorry, darling," said Mary absently, as she handed him the sugar bowl. "This wasn't funny, though. It was absolutely real, as real as this breakfast, Ted. Honestly, it was. He sat in that chair and I was at my table doing accounts with Tabby on my knee. He—he'd pricked his finger on the rose tree over the porch—"

"Always did do that," Ted admitted.

"Yes, I know, but it's what he said that's important. It's—it's about Andrew. He said he'd seen the people in charge of him and—"

"But your father's—"

"Yes, I know," interrupted Mary. "But the point is that he said Andrew was better. And he might be, you know. They said there was just—"

"One chance in a thousand," Ted said regretfully. "Doesn't do to kid yourself, darling."

"Yes, but they didn't say there wasn't just that one."

"That's true."

"Ted," said Mary suddenly, "if we find out that he really is better, that he's regained consciousness, will you take what else Daddy said seriously?"

"Well, I'd be more inclined to," Ted admitted.

"Will you ring up the Home and find out?"

Ted looked down at his plate. "Look here, can't I finish breakfast first?"

Mary laughed. "Of course. I'm being silly, I know. But it felt so real and it'd be so wonderful if it were. And I want you to ring instead of me because it'd be so much more convincing for you. And I just—daren't, to be quite honest."

Ted grinned. "All right. I'll ring them as soon as I've cleared this lot on my plate. There's nothing I'd like to hear more, as a matter of fact. Andrew's a grand chap. Look here, if there's anything in this hunch of yours, shall we have him here once they let him go?"

Mary looked awed. "But in my dream that's just what Daddy said Andrew wanted us to do. Whatever gave you the idea?"

"Dunno. Just think he's a good chap. Probably nothing in this theory that he's come round, though."

"Oh, but there is! There is!" Mary said.

"All right," said Ted. "We'll see." He finished his toast, tipped down the rest of his coffee, and rose.

Mary sat still at the breakfast table, hands clasped, excitement subsiding into stillness as she watched Ted cross the room in half a dozen strides to open the door into the hall. He looked so big in a house. Out of doors he seemed to match the other large-size things, like oak trees and shire horses; but in a house made by punier human beings he was always having to stoop, to negotiate, to adapt himself good-naturedly to the dimensions of lesser men. But being Ted he never seemed to mind. He was used to it. As he had once explained, he had to do the same sort of thing at sea, since destroyers didn't offer all that much headroom to men of six foot three.

Mary listened. Now he had picked up the receiver and asked for the number of the Home. It was a cross-country call. There might be quite a bit of delay. Mary watched the cat creep across a patch of shaded lawn, a shadow among the shadows, heard a blue-bottle buzzing and banging itself against the mysterious, invisible barrier of glass. Someone had answered. Ted was making inquiries in his usual voice, steady with the latent strength of so many terse commands. Then there was another pause. They must have asked if he would like to speak to the Superintendent, for Ted had said that he certainly would. That meant there was news... one way or another... perhaps good news....

Mary felt she must have waited half a lifetime. Yet the cat was only just emerging from the shadow, swift as malevolence, but not swift enough, for the menaced blackbird had taken flight with its harshly warning shriek. Then she heard Ted's voice again. Now it was different. He was astonished. Almost awed. He agreed to do something. Were they suggesting he should go and see Andrew for himself? That morning? He would be along right away. Then she heard the ping of the receiver being gently replaced on its hook.

Ted came back to the breakfast room and went straight to his blazer to look for his cigarette case. Mary managed to wait till he had got a cigarette going. And then she could wait no more.

"Well?" she asked.

"He's come round all right," said Ted slowly. "Just as you said."

"And is he talking?"

"Yes."

"Normally?"

"As far as they can tell."

"Oh, Ted! We can have him here?"

"Well, of course, they want to keep him under observation for a bit. This may be a temporary improvement. They've got to be sure."

"Oh dear, what nonsense!" Mary said. "Surely they've got enough experience by now to know when a man's sane and when he's not?"

"Well, it's been such a queer business altogether. Apparently he's utterly different. They can't make it out. And of course they don't want to raise our hopes too soon. Dash it all, Mary, he was right off his nut, they said."

"But that was only just because he'd—he'd retreated from life because he couldn't bear it," Mary said. "Daddy explained all that. He knows where he is now, does he? Andrew, I mean."

"They say so. At least he knows he's in the hospital. And his great idea is to get out, quick."

"Of course it is. How soon can he come here?"

"That's what I want to go and discuss. They said there were certain formalities—"

"Oh, lord! Formalities!"

"Well, there's bound to be quite a bit of red tape, you know, that they've got to get unsnarled before they can let him go. Since we're relations and willing to have him it mayn't be so bad. He can be under observation. Any way, I'll go right along in the car and see what's what."

"Shall I come too?" Mary asked.

Ted took two or three pulls at his cigarette before he answered her. "Think you'd better not," he said at last. "Stay here and get things fixed up for him. I don't suppose for a minute that I'll just be able to open the car door and tell him to get in."

"No, of course not," Mary agreed. "But I might as well have his room ready. Just in case...."

"That's the idea. Now the only other thing is, how's he off for cash? Will he need a bit to start him off? If so I'd better fix something with the Bank before I go back. He went straight from Oundrow to the Army in 1914, didn't he? Never had a job or a technical training? His pension'll stop if he's cured."

Mary said: "Yes, of course. But he's got a small income. Same as mine. We both got it at twenty-one from Granny."

"Good. I just wanted to be sure he wasn't going to be landed with nothing in his pockets. Rotten start, that. Gets a man down. Well, here we go."

A rakish little beast, largely Sealyham, emerged from under the breakfast table, as if it knew that the moment for action had come. In obvious triumph it led the way to the door while Ted slung on his blazer, filled his cigarette case from a box on Mary's writing table, kissed her and went out with his dog.

"I must say you don't waste much time in telling me how remarkably right I was," Mary said as she followed him to the front door.

"Didn't find it remarkable. You often are," Ted said, over his shoulder. Then he swung round the corner of the tall box hedge that hid the garage with Scrubby so close to his heels that he seemed liable to be kicked at every step.

Mary stood in the doorway, sniffing up the smell of the hot box hedge and listening to Ted starting up the car. After he had gone she still stood there, looking about her, trying to imagine what the world would seem like to Andrew when he saw it again with eyes that had so long been turned into the past. What must it be like, she wondered, to be Andrew, looking at reality after three years among shadows? Or hadn't they been like shadows? What could they have been like? They said people went out of their minds, but if you were out of your mind, yet still alive, where had you gone?

And what, she asked herself presently, was it going to be like to come back? To come back now, when things had already begun to go wrong? The men who'd returned in 1918 already knew it hadn't worked out according to the blueprints of a new world that they'd drawn up together in the trenches. But Andrew... Andrew would come back in the mood of 1915, when all things still seemed possible, even the brotherhood of man. What would Andrew make of the world of 1920, Mary wondered, as she picked up the cat which was leaning itself against her legs and considered what she ought to do next. Common sense told her that Ted couldn't possibly just put Andrew into the car and bring him back to lunch. Nevertheless she couldn't resist going upstairs and beginning preparations for installing him in the big spare room in which she had been dumping oddments ever since the last visitor had left.

Apart from the removal of such extras as cardboard boxes, broken chairs waiting to be mended, and the sewing machine, it would have to be thoroughly cleaned by Bertha, the little housemaid who was "learning" at the Cherry Orchard, under the stern supervision of her mother, Mrs. Burns, who was the cook. Obviously, Mary told herself, as she stood in the middle of the big, untidy room, the only result of taking Bertha off her routine work and getting her suddenly to turn out the spare bedroom would be to fluster her almost to a standstill. And so, with the date of Andrew's arrival still uncertain, the problem could be best dealt with in a leisurely way and in consultation with Mrs. Burns when she settled the day's meals. Accordingly, leaving the spare room rather more chaotic than she had found it, Mary went downstairs to have a word with Mrs. Burns.

That done, she wandered into the garden again in unreasonable expectation. Could the sound of a car's engine mean that Ted was back already? But it turned out to be only the butcher's van, and so she went round the house to the sand pit, where three-year-old Michael, fair, square and sturdy as his Scottie pup, was building a series of castles which the dog industriously tore down. Both boy and dog were plastered with wet sand to the ears and breathless with delight. Mary had come to watch, but after she had sent the nurse indoors she remained to enjoy herself, so that, when Ted drove up, a couple of hours later, his wife was completely unaware of his presence till she glanced up through the haze of sand to find him looking quizzically down on them from the edge of the lawn.

"Oh, Ted, you're back at last!" She scrambled out, shaking particles from her dress and hair. "Tell me quick. What's the news? When can he come?"

"Well, he can't come right away, darling. Not just like that," said Ted, preparing to rekindle his pipe. "We knew that, didn't we?"

"Yes." But Mary's voice was so flat with disappointment that Ted had to smile.

"What a kid you are sometimes, love. And sometimes so wise."

"How is he, though?" asked Mary urgently. "What did you think?"

"I thought it was a ruddy miracle, as a matter of fact," said Ted. "He's just the very same as he was before he got that knock in 1915. Can't remember a thing after that, you know. He's like someone who's just wakened up."

"I know," Mary said. "Daddy told me that, last night."

Ted looked at her uncomfortably. "Well, anyhow," he said, "there it is."

"And when can he come?"

"Not for some weeks, at least," Ted said. "He'll have to be kept under observation till they're satisfied that this isn't just a lucid interval, apparently."

"And then?"

"Then the Medical Officer does his stuff and he comes out on probation. That lasts a year, with periodic inspections. Quarterly, I think. Just routine. Dr. Ward can do them. By the way, oughtn't you to let your mother know?"

"She won't want Andrew at the Grange," Mary said. "It's the Red Cross headquarters, and dear knows what else. Mother just lives for her committees, nowadays. And Andrew'd loathe it."

"But there's going to be trouble if she isn't told."

Mary nodded. "I'd better telephone her right away."

She set off towards the house, brushing the rest of the sand off her frock.

Mrs. Prothero had emerged from the war with a high rank and suitable decorations recognizing the value of her work for the Red Cross, and was now quite unable to bear the idea of dismantling her headquarters at the Grange. So its drawing rooms were still devoted to various committees, its billiard room to lectures, its library and morning room remained offices for herself and the assistants who were engaged in various branches of women's work, social and political, which she sponsored. Consequently her lofty rooms remained austere and scrubbed, curtainless and stacked with files, at a time when most other people's big houses had already reverted to carpets and brocades.

It was in the library, behind the big desk which was covered with overflowing wire baskets, that Mrs. Prothero, plump, iron-grey and prodigiously efficient, received Mary's call. It came at an awkward moment, just as she had begun to dictate a batch of correspondence, so that she had to send her secretary on an errand and switch from international affairs to this startling development in her own. Of course it was wonderful news... but so sudden! So sudden... she gripped the edge of her desk... and how tiresome, how difficult, everything was going to be! Mr. Prothero had been right when he said his wife was secretly terrified of any sort of abnormality. She had managed to avoid thinking of Andrew for months, almost for years. And now....

"He's actually leaving the home? He's better? Quite normal? Has Ted really spoken to him? But... that means... how can I undertake the responsibility? What's to happen to all my work?"

Her usually measured voice had an almost shrill note in it which Mr. Prothero would have recognized. Her pale blue eyes glanced here and there like those of a creature which fancies itself trapped.

"You—you and Ted want to have him? On probation? Well..." She let out her breath on a long, wavering sigh. Her relief was evident, and, in that commanding figure, also pathetic. "I suppose that might be possible. Your nursing experience? H'm. Not much in that. If it were not for my commitments I should never dream of allowing... but there it is. I cannot possibly set them aside for merely personal considerations. After all—we are an international—a world-wide organization. I feel the work must come first."

She allowed herself to be soothed by Mary's quiet assurance. "Well, I suppose it's all right. When is he to come to you? You don't really know anything yet? I see. Well, you must let me know immediately he arrives. I shall come and see him, of course. Yes. Definitely. Meanwhile, my secretary is waiting... some urgent correspondence...."

Mary sighed as she put the receiver back on its hook. Poor Mother. It was so impossible not to see through all that pomp. If she could ever bring herself to admit that she was just scared stiff, how much easier it would be. Well, the next thing was to get Andrew. And how long was that going to take?

It took, actually, only a few weeks for Andrew to be passed as fit to go home, and when formalities were completed he was told that Mary and Ted would fetch him in the car next day. That night sleep remained remote, but it mattered less to Andrew now that all life had taken on the colors of a dream. He lay with his hands clasped behind his head and his eyes on the pale oblong of window across which the stately constellations swung as the hours passed and the world turned towards morning. Inside the converted mansion which was the Officers' Home the night's quiet was occasionally broken by the creaking steps of a nurse, the flap of a blind, the cry of someone struggling with a nightmare. But outside the window, wide-flung but barred, the stillness was profound, exquisite, only enhanced, not shattered, by the sounds that belonged to the night.

As he lay awake Andrew was remembering that first talk with Ted, some weeks ago now, and thinking how much the war years of authority had changed his brother-in-law, giving him a gravity and poise which made him feel so much younger and less experienced by comparison. Of course Ted hadn't put on any side. He'd been just the same, decent and inarticulate, as he'd always been. And he'd sounded as if he really wanted Andrew to come to the Cherry Orchard.

Mary was lucky. Ted's face had changed when he spoke of her, and something in his expression had touched an answering chord that echoed almost like a memory. And yet, Andrew told himself, he couldn't really know how Ted felt. Nobody had ever meant to him what Mary meant to Ted. But all the same, he did know how Ted felt. And Mary—well, there wasn't anyone to touch her in the world.

Andrew smiled at the memory of old Ted sitting there by his bedside, his face puckered with his anxiety to give exact answers to the stream of questions that he, Andrew, had poured out. A funny thing, he'd fancied at one point that Ted was almost nervous in case he was going to be asked something that he wouldn't know how to answer. But perhaps that was just his imagination. Old Ted never did like being made to talk, from the days when he'd almost as soon face a firing squad as an examiner.

Andrew found himself trying to puzzle out some of Ted's answers; what he'd said about his father, for instance. It was queer, that. Somewhere at the back of his mind were other memories, quite recent ones, of meetings with his father in which he looked alert and well. It didn't seem to match Ted's talk of a lingering illness during which he'd shut himself up in London and seen next to nobody. His father hadn't looked ill when he'd come to see him in the hospital. (Not this place. Somewhere else.) Dash it all, he'd been at the top of his form. It had been his father's idea that he should go and stay with Ted and Mary as soon as they'd let him go. Andrew frowned into the thinning darkness, trying to regain the memory. His father had said...had said...but here he lost the track of memories so elusive that they slid away from him as minnows elude a small boy's outspread, over-eager hands.

Then at last, tired enough to abandon further speculation, Andrew began to doze, to drift, to lose himself among the tantalizingly half-familiar shapes of shallow dreams till the morning light crept across his quietened face.

Mary had not told Michael that Andrew was coming to stay. She'd had to tell too many people that her brother, who'd had shell-shock, was better, and coming to them for a while. She'd told the friends and neighbors whom she met in and out of the village shops. She'd told the servants, the vicar and the doctor. She'd told Michael's young and rather frighteningly efficient nurse. And now she felt she couldn't bear one more question about Andrew, not even from Michael himself. The casual, non-committal answers she forced herself to give expressed so little of the intense, protective love she felt for Andrew, the same sort of brooding, fundamental feeling she would have if something had threatened Michael or Ted, that now reached out to enfold Andrew with her instinctive compassion because he needed to be guarded and understood.

She gave no indication of her feelings as Ted turned the car in at the gates of the Cherry Orchard, swung round the corner by the box hedge and drew up in front of the door. Only Michael knew that something important had happened to his mother as soon as she swept him up off the doorstep on which he had appeared at the sound of the car. He could feel something different from her usual warm tranquility. He knew, child as he was, that the pace of life which cradled him so softly had quickened, that both his parents were stirred, even afraid. It made him feel a little anxious as he looked at the stranger to whom his mother had turned just a little too exuberantly, saying:

"Well, Andrew, what d'you think of this?"

"We haven't done much to the place really," Ted was saying, as he reached for Andrew's case. "It won't seem strange."

But though they had opened the door for him Andrew still sat in the car. He looked gravely about him, his face awed as he saw again after his years of outer darkness the beauty of brick and lichen, rose alley and sturdy apple trees, while Michael, equally grave, watched the stranger intently from his mother's arms.

"Wake up, Andrew, this is Michael," said Mary at last.

Andrew turned his head slowly, as if he could scarcely bear to lose sight of a single aspect of the homely place about him. Then he encountered Michael's steady eyes. They looked at each other gravely, tall man and tiny boy, for what seemed a very long time. Each was aware, in some oddly direct way, of a kinship which was not only of the flesh but inherent in a mutual need for things that other people valued too lightly, perhaps most of all in the sense of wonder that they shared. Then at last, as if on the same impulse, they smiled....

Mr. Prothero blinked at the sunlight filtering down on him through the clusters of rambler roses, crimson, pink and white, which poured over rustic trellis-work. He shifted a little on the wooden bench and smiled contentedly. He was back on his favorite seat at the end of the rose alley at the Cherry Orchard again. The westering sunlight touched his face, patterned his shoulders, fell gently on his hands, loosely clasped between his knees in a favorite attitude as he leaned forward and looked down the vista of chevroned brick paving towards the house. He was expecting Andrew to come along. Somehow or other, he had the idea that Andrew knew he was there and would come out to see him presently. He would be glad to have a word with Andrew, just to be sure that things were going well. It was pleasant there in the rose alley, so pleasant that Mr. Prothero waited without impatience. He had no idea how long it was before Andrew appeared in the distance; Andrew as he had once never dared to hope that he would see him again; Andrew, brown-faced and happy, smiling down at the small boy who trotted beside him, babbling excitedly in a bat-like squeak.

"Well, Andrew," said Mr. Prothero, as they reached his bench, "I hoped you'd come. Did they tell you I was here?"

"I—knew," Andrew said. "Somehow or other." He sat down on the sun-warmed bench, and held out a hand to the child. "Good to see you, Dad. Remember Mary's baby? Isn't he getting a big chap? Like to come up, Michael?"

But Michael shook his head. He was standing sturdily in front of them, feet astride, hands deep in the pockets of his green linen shorts, his brown face puckered with inquiry as he stared up at Mr. Prothero.

"I'm Michael," he said eventually. "Who're you?"

"That's Grandfather," Andrew explained.

"Oh," Michael continued to stare. Mr. Prothero felt slightly at a loss, aware of being assessed minutely by this deliberate child. It was a long time since he had had any dealings with children. He was not sure what his grandson would expect. Their vocabularies were widely divergent; he never had had any baby talk. Then, tentatively, he twitched his moustache and managed to make what had always been known as his "rabbit-face" in the days when Mary and Andrew had been in turn convulsed by it. Michael responded immediately. His critical expression relaxed into delight. Throwing himself on Mr. Prothero, he pounded his knees and squealed with laughter.

"Rabbit, rabbit!" he shouted. "Do it again!"

And so, from that instant, Mr. Prothero's conversation with Andrew was punctuated with imperious demands from Michael, who doubled himself up with appreciation, and only recovered to demand that Mr. Prothero should do it again.

Andrew, it seemed, had never been so happy anywhere as at the Cherry Orchard. Ted had asked him to stay on and manage the property. It didn't amount to much yet, for most of the land had been let off for grazing, but there were good farm buildings, and a few cows and pigs would do for a start. Andrew liked the idea of learning about stock and land. Mr. Prothero listened to his plans with real pleasure. They were sensible, wary, and well-defined. "Of course I've got to feel my way," Andrew explained. "The local chaps are pretty decent, though, as long as I don't give the impression that I'm above taking advice."

Mr. Prothero asked questions, liked the sound of all he heard. As he talked, Andrew's eyes grew dreamy, and he began blissfully to map out the future, when he, and Michael too if he were interested, would expand from small-holding to farm, from a few cows and chickens and pigs to a flourishing milk herd and poultry yard, when the empty cowsheds and barns would be full again and the Cherry Orchard once more the center of fifty acres of well-tilled land.

"I've everything to learn, of course."

"So long as you know that," said Mr. Prothero, "you'll come to no harm."

"Well, I look at it this way, . . ." said Andrew.

Attentive, appreciative, critical, Mr. Prothero let him run on. He had a fancy as he listened to Andrew's eager, enthusiastic talk, watching his eyes, in which awe at his good fortune still gravely lingered, that so Lazarus might have looked and spoken, had there been any possibility of truth in the story of a man who had been raised from the dead. Lazarus would not have been able to explain, any more than Andrew could. But he too would . . . Mr. Prothero narrowed his eyes and sought for a simile . . . he too would almost have glowed.

Time meant so little to him these days that it was a surprise when Andrew rose. "Got to be going, I'm afraid, Dad. Coming, old chap?"

But Michael lingered, fists pounding his grandfather's knee.

"Come again, Grandfather?"

"I'll come again."

"Promise?"

"I promise I will."

"Often, though. Often?"

"As often," said Mr. Prothero, "as I possibly can."

CHAPTER 7

The director reached the end of a descriptive monologue and paused. "Well, that's the principle behind the work of the psycho-therapeutic department. I'd like you to meet the students who're in charge of the Cherry Orchard quite soon. You'll be interested, I think. It's part of their job, you see, to study the conditions surrounding the people there so that they can anticipate crisis-points in plenty of time."

"It sounds," said Mr. Prothero, "a most comprehensive scheme. Like—like a panel of guardian angels." He laughed at his little joke.

But the director merely nodded. "People used to take their help for granted," he said. "Nowadays only a few people are prepared to believe that they exist at all. Here, of course, we are in a rather better position to estimate the possibilities. Ministering spirits, you remember, were also mentioned. They have discarded them too. And yet—"

"Spirits?" said Mr. Prothero doubtfully. "I dislike the word. Ethereal, it sounds. Wispy...."

"The men and women who work here are certainly neither ethereal nor wispy," the director said. "I suggest you reassure yourself about that at once. It's time you met the people you'll be working with. James Grant will take you to the observation rooms. I expect you'll find him waiting for you outside."

He rose and held out his hand. Mr. Prothero was aware of his firm, hard clasp. Certainly the director at least was neither ethereal nor wispy. "Don't hesitate to come and have a word with me at any time. I'm never too busy," he said.

James Grant was in the corridor. "Shall we go to the general observation room, then?" he said, as if he had overheard the conversation, "since you're to meet the people who look after the Cherry Orchard and see how your work's going to fit in."

"I should like that very much," said Mr. Prothero, wondering as he spoke whether he was in for another of those high-speed-lift effects in which James Grant seemed to specialize. He was aware of a certain reluctance to encounter the experts who would, inevitably, consider him a back number and a nuisance. So he was glad that they did not take a lift, but merely strolled along the corridor and up a flight of stairs to the floor above, where they walked past a number of wards towards a pair of swing-doors at the far end.

As James Grant swung these aside and held back a curtain, Mr. Prothero went slowly into the strangest room he had ever seen. It was very large, circular, and windowless. The smooth walls seemed to be made of illuminated glass, which gave a series of translucent pictures of the continents of the world. Across them multicolored light swept and shimmered from sea to sea, till its vivid alternations seemed to make the whole room pulsate. Mr. Prothero stood just inside the door, blinking as the colored lights on the wall swept to and fro, waxing or waning from moment to moment, occasionally encountering a conflicting wave in vivid flashes of explosive radiance which were carefully noted by the men and women in white coats or overalls who were grouped round the big room, their faces absorbed as they watched the glowing colors change.

"That's a revolution in Mexico," said James Grant, as a vivid flash made Mr. Prothero jump. "And those are the troubles in Ireland." He pointed out a throbbing, sullen glow to the west of the British Isles which gave off a series of threatening sparks. "There's a nasty problem boiling up in Germany too. Look, over there. Those people are checking up on it." He pointed to a group of young men and women who were watching a slow, weary convulsion of phosphorescently unhealthy color which looked like a motion-picture speed-up of the process of suppuration. "The light is nearly out. You can see how the shadows of sepsis are creeping in and smothering it. The people watching have got case work in that part of Europe. I don't wonder they're vexed."

Mr. Prothero was too astonished to be coherent. "You mean to tell me that... this can't be... a sort of recording apparatus...?"

"For the emotional state of every country in the world? Exactly," said James Grant. "Don't ask me to explain how it works, for even television is only just reaching the scientists over yonder, so ye've got nothing to go by yet. Dramatic, ihmhm. Eh, but sometimes it's like a sort of cosmic bonfire. Ye can see for yourself what a lot of unrest's going on now, how greed's frustrating everybody's hopes. Those points that look like exploding bubbles... there... in England and France and Germany and central Europe—yon's strikes. Transport workers... miners... dockers... factory hands. Yon sort of firework business that looks like an oxyacetylene drill at work is the young Soviet Union eating its way into the old order. Aye, and there's trouble coming over there, as well." He pointed to another wall. "Yonder's America. Look how the light's flickering in the industrial areas. Trouble's due there, by the end of the 'twenties, I'd say."

Mr. Prothero turned to follow James Grant's pointing finger. He saw a silent group of students, notebooks in hand, who were watching the convulsions of ugly, clashing, greedy color which swept across the North American continent. The faces of the attentive young men and women were grave, like those of a group of students studying a patient's fever chart, and the fiery lights from the wall lit up their faces as if they were standing by an open furnace door.

"Extraordinary," murmured Mr. Prothero. "The whole place is churning about like molten lava."

James Grant nodded. "Aye, it's an eruptive period. Some folk here think it'll get worse and worse till western civilization fair destroys itself and younger life seeps in from the unsophisticated areas in the east. I don't agree. I think there's going to be an appalling crisis and a last-minute recovery from what looks like extinction in the west."

"It hurts my eyes to look at it," said Mr. Prothero.

"Ihmhm, it's too cosmic to watch for long," agreed James Grant. "We all come here to get a wider view that corrects our detailed work, but I agree with ye. Ye can easy have too much of it. It's awful Wagnerian. I'd rather deal with folk myself. Come next door. It's daylight there, for a start, and that's a lot easier on the eyes."

Mr. Prothero followed him thankfully, through the other swing-doors at the far end, into another great hall, also full of students. But open casement windows ran down the two sides, with wide, cushioned window-seats on which people were gossiping or looking out on the gardens below. Other people were busy with notebooks at long tables which were ranged down the center of the room, or fetching volumes from shelves which formed alcoves within which smaller tables were set. It might have been the library of any university, thought Mr. Prothero. Overwhelmed as he still was by the awful scope of the gigantic recording apparatus, he began to feel a little better.

"I'd like you to have a word with Hugh," said James Grant, as he led the way towards a group who seemed to be working together at a round table in one of the alcoves. "Hugh's been looking after Andrew. And this is Laura. She's been helping Mary, especially since Michael was born. And Giles here has been detailed to keep an eye on Ted. This is Mr. Prothero," said James Grant as they paused by the table.

Mr. Prothero was surprised by the cordiality of the three young people who immediately made a place for him at the round table. He found himself sitting between Laura and Giles, explaining how anxious he had been about Andrew, how thankful when Mary and Ted offered him a home.

They listened so attentively that he took courage. He had never expected more than their toleration, or perhaps a sort of reluctant co-operation induced by official command. But they seemed actually glad to have him there, to count on his help, to want his ideas. He was only an ordinary, prosy old man, Mr. Prothero reminded himself. How should he be welcome to the young?

"But of course," said the tawny-haired girl called Laura, as if he had spoken aloud. Flustered, Mr. Prothero looked at her again. An elusive sense of familiarity puzzled him.

"Haven't I seen you before?" he asked.

"Yes, often," said Laura, pushing back her short curls. She was plump and rather small. Her eyes were brown and she had a wide, curling smile. "I used to be Mary's greatest friend at school. I was always in and out of the Grange in the holidays. I'm Laura Ward, and my people are at the Old Mill now."

"Of course," said Mr. Prothero. "You and Mary, always together—"

"And Hugh." Laura nodded across the table at the tall boy with brown eyes and thin, mobile features. "He was going to marry my sister, Joanna, you know."

"I'm afraid it isn't awfully clear in my mind," said Mr. Prothero, teased by a drifting thread of memory. Hadn't something happened to those Wards, something that upset Mrs. Ward so much that her husband thought a new home necessary to take her mind off it? Something... something like a motoring accident... a boy and girl... unforeseen tragedy at a holiday picnic party? Hadn't it been just before Mary got married? Just before the Wards moved to the Old Mill? He couldn't remember. He returned to the question in hand.

"Well, about Andrew and the Cherry Orchard," he said. "If you really think I can help...."

"You certainly can," Laura said. "They mayn't be able to remember the things you tell them afterwards, but you'll probably find that Mary, at any rate, will often take your advice without knowing why. He might even make some impression on Ted, Giles, don't you think?"

Giles grinned. He was a sturdy, heavily-built young man with very blue eyes under level black brows and ears that rather stood out from his head. "Nobody makes much impression on Ted," he said. "He's a really tough proposition, you can take it from me." Mr. Prothero found himself liking Giles. He could imagine him having a lot in common with Ted, but more sense of humor.

"You see, the worst of it is that I've got to keep out of sight so much. Whenever Ted sees me he thinks he's having a nightmare. It's all very well for you people to laugh," he protested, "but I was posted missing at sea in 1914, and poor old Ted thinks I went down with my ship and that was the end of that. I can't make him believe that it wasn't."

"Well, couldn't I tell him you didn't? Go down with the ship, I mean," said Mr. Prothero.

They smiled at him. "It isn't as simple as that," Hugh explained.

Mr. Prothero looked at Hugh with attention. He was taller than the others, with freckles across a snub nose and widely set grey eyes.

"But I can tell him you're perfectly well," said Mr. Prothero. He felt full of confidence now.

"If you could explain to my mother that I really am doing a useful job of work here, I'd be thankful," Laura said. "She hates my being away from home."

"But of course I'll go and see her when I'm at the Cherry Orchard," said Mr. Prothero. "You got a chance of coming to this hospital, where you're doing special work under most favorable conditions. It shouldn't be difficult. I can assure her that I've seen the place myself. She can't insist you ought to have stayed at home then."

"Not—if you can make her believe you, Mr. Prothero."

"But surely she'll believe me. I can tell her I've seen it all for myself."

"You can tell her, Mr. Prothero."

"You really think she won't believe me?"

"I don't know," Laura said. "Try and see."

"Maybe you could talk to Joanna at the same time, Mr. Prothero," said Hugh. "She had a nervous breakdown when I came here. She won't listen to me either. Or to Laura . . . she's her sister, you know. . . ."

"I'll talk to them with pleasure," Mr. Prothero said. He looked round the circle of young faces, glad to be able to offer to do something that would help people who had impressed him more than he cared to admit. They must make up a remarkable team, thought Mr. Prothero, as he looked from one to the other, recognizing in Giles a finely tempered resolution; guessing at Hugh's eager, imaginative zeal and Laura's deep compassion, appreciating James Grant's deliberate, philosophic mind. He noticed, too, that though they were grave enough about the work itself, they teased each other unmercifully about lesser things. Between them went a continual shimmer of amiable nonsense, the small change of trusted friends. Yes, they made a good, a remarkably good team, Mr. Prothero told himself, whatever the nature of their work might be.

"Well, after all," he said, just a little complacently, "you might find that I made a different impression on your mother, you know. People are apt to forget that their children grow up and strike out on their own. I'll certainly look in at the Old Mill and reassure your mother, Laura. I expect she'll take my word for it. And Joanna, yes, I'll have a word with her too. That should put things right, don't you think?"

"I hope so," Laura said. Her voice was doubtful, but she smiled at Mr. Prothero, who was now struggling to express the beginnings of a grievance. "The trouble is," he said, "I'm a surgeon. I must say I'd hoped to be given work nearer my own line rather than be left to study this—this psycho-therapeutic stuff."

"It's a funny thing, Mr. Prothero," said James Grant, breaking abruptly into the conversation, "how many different qualifications can land ye in the same place over here. Take Hugh: he used to be a radiologist."

"I was in mine-sweepers," said Giles.

"I was just a V.A.D.," said Laura.

"We've got a chap who used to run a flying circus," said Hugh. "And another who worked on the railways. There's a couple of padres, an Arctic explorer, a circus acrobat and a music-hall queen in our show, too. Different jobs, dear knows. But we've all landed up in the psycho-therapeutic department, just the same."

"Yes, but why?" Mr. Prothero frowned and pondered.

Giles shook his head. Hugh raised his eyebrows. James Grant shrugged. Laura said: "You all know, but you'd rather I said it, just in case it sounds sissy. Words are such clumsy things if you aren't clever with them. And none of us are. It's something to do with the way we feel about people, Mr. Prothero. We'd express it in melody if we were musicians or in color if we were artists, with a special way of getting things across. We can't use their symbols, because we aren't artists, so we try to get in touch with people direct. I suppose that everyone in the psycho-therapeutic department has to have a certain knack for detecting other people's gifts and fostering them. We're only beginners, of course, but we can't help feeling that it's the most interesting work of all. Can you see that it might be?"

"Yes," said Mr. Prothero doubtfully. "I suppose I can. But——" He broke off rather helplessly; he felt out of his depth among abstractions. His work had been so clear-cut, precise as the keen edge of one of his own instruments, shadowless as one of the powerful lights above his operating table. He was ill at ease among the subtleties of the imagination. All this talk, this talk...it was interesting enough, no doubt, but it seemed irrelevant. He found it hard to keep his mind on it for long. Odd. He'd been proud of his ability to concentrate. Now, as soon as he let his will relax into quiescence his attention drifted away, as it seemed to have got into the way of doing just lately, on a wave of longing for familiar things, towards the Cherry Orchard. He found himself wondering about them all, picturing the simple routine of their life, reaching towards them with tenderness and hope....

Almost at once he was aware of that sinking feeling he had come to associate with the oddly obliterated journeys which he had been making lately and could remember so little about. Then came the sensation of warmth, the warmth of the westering sun on his shoulders, and the hardness of the wood of his favorite seat at the end of the rose alley against back and thighs. He looked about him, surprised but lazily content.

A small boy in grey shorts and a vivid shirt was standing quite near him, practising with a homemade catapult which he didn't seem to know much about. His floppy linen hat partly hid a face which was grave and preoccupied till suddenly he spun round with a yelp, sucking a bruised thumb and dancing with pain.

"Tch, tch," said Mr. Prothero. "I used to do that. It hurts, doesn't it?"

Michael took his thumb out of his mouth and grinned. One of his front teeth was missing. How absurdly fast all children grew.

"Hullo, Grandfather. It doesn't hurt much now. I'm glad you've come."

"Good," said Mr. Prothero. "How's everybody?"

"They're all right. Bertha's supposed to be looking after me, but I can give her the slip as quick as quick. Andrew made me this catapult. But there's something wrong with the way it works, the nasty thing."

"There's quite a lot wrong with the way you're holding it," said Mr. Prothero. "Give it to me."

"All right," Michael said.

Mr. Prothero held out his hand, but as he took the catapult a rush of memories seemed to pour over him, so that reality was submerged beneath their tide. His own first catapult...made by the gardener's boy...the catapult that had been confiscated during his second term at school...the other catapult he himself had made for Andrew when he'd been just about Michael's age.... As his fingers settled into the old grip round the pale, peeled hazel stem, striped with knife-cuts, he could no longer tell one from another, or indeed be sure whether the catapult he now held had something of the substance of them all, drawing its reality, not from one specific contraption of leather, rubber and wood, but from something more durable, something from which they had each been in turn derived, something that variously expressed itself in the eager lawlessness of boyhood, the fierce primitive desire to seek, pursue and kill that had its roots far back in the past.

Mr. Prothero did not so much consciously know these things as feel the knowledge of them flow through him, as he fingered the catapult, in great waves of awareness which he could neither check nor control. But eventually Michael's high voice roused him again.

"Go on, Grandfather," he demanded. "Show me how."

"This is the place for your thumb, you see," said Mr. Prothero, dreamily. "Your fingers curl round here. Now fit the stone in. That's right. Now pull...."

Michael's sturdy figure braced itself, tense with effort. His lower lip jutted out. He screwed up his eyes as he drew back the thongs to the limit of their elasticity, then suddenly relaxed as the stone sang overhead.

"Better, isn't it?" said Mr. Prothero.

"Much better," Michael said. "You do it now."

"You do it again," said Mr. Prothero.

"All right," Michael agreed. Then, after a while, he paused. "Grandfather, why are you only visiting us? Why don't you stay here all the time?"

"Because I've got work to do, old chap. Somewhere else," explained Mr. Prothero.

"Oh. D'you like that?"

"Very much."

"Oh. What sort of work?"

"Work in a hospital," said Mr. Prothero.

"You don't look ill."

"Other people are, though. This is a place where they try out all sorts of new ideas. I shall have to start again, they tell me," said Mr. Prothero. "It'll be like going to school." He sighed.

"I shouldn't like that either," Michael said. "I don't want to go to school."

"Not ever?"

"Not ever. I'd rather stay here with Andrew and Hamish and Scrubby and the cows and Mummy. For always, I mean. Right up to when I'm a big man."

"You'd get a bit tired of that, I expect," said Mr. Prothero.

"No, I shouldn't. Tell me about the place you work in, now."

"Well..." Mr. Prothero considered the question, closing his eyes for better concentration. "It's difficult to describe...." He spoke dreamily, conscious at first of the weight of Michael's head on his shoulder, the warmth of his usually restless body, now stilled within the curve of his protecting arm. But as he tried to find words with which to describe the hospital he began to lose contact with Michael, to talk less to the child than to himself, arguing vigorously with certain rebellious elements in his own mind.

How could he describe the place to anyone? He neither knew where it was nor how he'd ever got there. Then why not go to the authorities and ask for an explanation? Surely that was what any man in his senses would immediately do? Any man in his senses... Mr. Prothero nerved himself to face the suspicion which had been troubling him. Had he, like Andrew, gone out of his mind?

He opened his eyes and looked round him in sudden terror. Where was he now, for instance? In the rose alley at the Cherry Orchard? No, he was sitting on a bench in the hospital grounds, for in the distance the walls of the great structure rose like cliffs with the warmth of the sunset on them. Mr. Prothero groaned, shaking his head as if to dislodge the delusive memory of a conversation with Michael. Undoubtedly he was in a very strange mental state.

If he reported these periodic blackouts to the hospital authorities... perhaps they might not let him work. Perhaps they would consider that he ought to be put under restraint. Like Andrew. Mr. Prothero recoiled from the nightmare memory. Better, much better, dead. For death at least offered the mercy of complete extinction. At least... a very strange thought crossed Mr. Prothero's mind for a fleeting instant, to be discarded almost instantaneously. Death was extinction. It could be nothing else. Therefore while he himself still spoke, heard, moved, obviously he still lived. And mental derangement was something to be concealed, in self-defence, for as long as possible.

So much was mere common sense. But what of the future? Was this the beginning of a total breakdown? Was his condition improving, or was it getting worse?

"One thing I know, whereas I was blind, now I see."

The words impinged on his mind. He supposed they had been spoken close at hand, looking wildly round him for the speaker. He was in a part of the grounds which was apparently being reclaimed from thorns and scrub, alone except for a man in the distance whom he supposed to be the gardener, busy with his work. Had the gardener spoken? Mr. Prothero could not tell. But the words themselves had been true enough. He had been nearly blind, a back number. Now, apart from these intermittent blackouts, he felt like a youngster again. Ready for anything. He had recently been taking part in a most interesting discussion, for instance, with a group of students. He remembered perfectly. In one of these new-fangled observation rooms. It should be simple enough to find them again.

As he rose, the gardener paused and looked at him. Mr. Prothero was aware of a sudden, almost electric sensation of shock. Nonsense, of course, sheer neurotic nonsense. He must get back to the others again....

They were still sitting round the table, just as they had been. James, who had been making a note on a scribbling pad, was still tapping his pencil against his front teeth. Hugh, who had been lifting his arms, had only just clasped his fingers behind his head. Laura was still balancing herself on the back legs of her chair. Mr. Prothero blinked, and while the room steadied about him he watched them finish the movements they had begun before he left.

Left? How could he have gone anywhere and returned in less time than Hugh took to clasp his hands or Laura to tilt her chair forward again? His brain had been playing more tricks. But nobody seemed to have noticed, fortunately. He could only have been unconscious for a few seconds, at most. Unconscious and dreaming, no more.

"Mind if I have a word with you, Giles?" A stranger had come up to the table, a smallish, rather precise-looking man whom he had not seen before.

"Sure," said Giles, swinging round. "Fire away, Pinkerton."

"Well, it's like this..." began Pinkerton, rubbing his nose. "I'm a bit bothered about a chap from our area...."

Giles listened intently for a while. Then he rose.

"Got to go to the special recording room," he said over his shoulder to the others. "There's trouble blowing up for us, I hear."

"Why don't ye come too, Mr. Prothero?" said James. "They'll screen the area for inspection. It'll mebbe interest ye to watch Giles and this other chap work the graph out. It's just through this way."

Obediently Mr. Prothero went with the others into another room which reminded him of his experiments in photography as a boy. Red lights glowed dimly here and there, and groups of people were standing in front of large luminous screens which were ruled off, numbered like gigantic temperature charts, in black and white, while lines in various contrasting colors crept from left to right, crossing and recrossing each other as they undulated up and down. Giles and the newcomer, Pinkerton, had paused before a screen near the door which clicked into visibility as they reached it. James Grant, hands in pockets, remained in the background, watching thoughtfully, but Laura came up to Mr. Prothero and laid a hand on his arm.

"I can tell you a bit about this," she said as they looked at the screen. "I came here when Mary nearly had an accident on Andrew's pony Pepper. We could see from the graph that there was almost certain to be trouble if she went for a ride with another girl who wasn't nearly as good on a horse as she thought she was. If they'd gone out that morning they'd have met a party of gypsies at a certain point, the other girl's pony would have bolted and Pepper would have swept Mary off against an oak tree as he set off to catch them up. But we managed to get the other girl to telephone and say that as it was so hot she'd rather they went for a swim. Such a little thing, but more important than it looked. You know how it is—people often say that something made them change their minds. Well, in certain circumstances we suggest such changes. But if other people are involved we've got to look at the whole pattern. And if they won't listen to us we may not interfere. Now here, for instance—"

Mr. Prothero looked at the bright screen in a bemused way. Wavy lines of colored light were creeping across it, over a background of subsidiary lines marked in black dots. "People are recorded in their dominant colors," Laura explained. "The deep blue line next to Ted's brick red is Mary, Andrew is green and Michael crimson. The dotted lines are people we're not concerned with at present. Here's where the trouble comes, you see. This yellow line belongs to somebody from another area who's crashing in—"

"An insurance broker from Birmingham on holiday in his racing car, I'm told," said Giles in a thoughtful voice. "He's liable to converge on the Cherry Orchard party in Ted's car at high speed, sometime tomorrow afternoon—"

"Looks to me just about three-thirty," said Pinkerton. "As far as I can work out the coefficients involved—"

"You know," said Giles judicially, after scribbling among his notes, "I'd still say it was near to three o'clock."

"Not if my chap stops off for lunch at a roadhouse," said Pinkerton. "If he just takes sandwiches I'll agree. But all the indications are that he's going to meet a certain lady, who's traveling from London by train, at Basingstoke, and she's going to insist on a proper meal. If it'd been sandwiches while driving I wouldn't have called you in, for they'd have quite a useful margin. But now—" He pursed his lips and frowned.

"Good heavens," exclaimed Mr. Prothero, "what sort of a place is this? You're not trying to tell me that you can forecast events that won't take place for another twenty-four hours?"

"We can plot their lines of probability, Mr. Prothero," Hugh explained. "You'd be surprised to find how seldom we're far out."

"But look at the speeds," objected Mr. Prothero, "A racing car—an express train—how can they be recorded as such snail's tracks as there?" He pointed to the slow, menacing convergence of a shrill pink line on the canary yellow which indicated the motorist from Birmingham, and their further convergence on the other colors which were looping leisurely forward, side by side.

"Well, you see, Mr. Prothero," explained Pinkerton in his painstaking way, "velocity is all a question of values, as far as we're concerned. Sometimes things here seem to race by clock-time standards, and sometimes to creep. Over the Border, for instance, they say a racing car driven at sixty miles an hour must obviously go faster than a donkey cart driven at six. But we say that all depends on the respective drivers' anxiety to reach their journeys' end. You think you've only been here a little while, don't you? But it's 1926 already over there."

Mr. Prothero scarcely heard him. All his attention was concentrated on the slow, threatening movements on the screen.

"I don't like the look of it, I must say," admitted Giles. "Can't you do anything to make your chap change his mind?"

Pinkerton shook his head. "He won't listen to a word until he's had a couple. He's really rather a nice chap then."

"Well, can't you get him to have a drink with this expensive meal?"

"Not a hope. The woman he's meeting has some violent prejudices. Against men who drink and drive cars, for instance. And he hasn't a chance of breaking it down till this evening. That's going to be too late for us."

"Who's looking after the woman from London?" asked Laura. "Can't we get on to the people in her area and see if they can produce a really good reason to keep her at home?"

"I've tried that," said Pinkerton, looking worried. "They report she won't listen at all. Her husband's neglecting her and she's decided she's now going to show him that two can play at that game. The reports list her as tough as a camel, as bold as brass, and just about as obstinate as a Brighton donkey."

"Dear me, she's certainly exasperated somebody," Laura said.

"I'll try working on Ted," said Giles. "But I know what he is when he gets an idea. It's about as easy to divert him as to stop water from running downhill."

"Failing Ted," said Hugh, "the rest of us had better get busy. Worst of it is that I don't want to bother Andrew any more for a bit. He ought to be left to settle down. He's nearly established now. What about Michael, though?"

"Bill's taking him on quite soon," said Laura. "He'll be a whole-time job when he goes to school. But Bill's still on an Air Force job. He's putting in work with a boy who used to be in the German Air Force and keeps trying to commit suicide to be with his pals. I wonder if Mary..."

Jane Oliver

"Good heavens," said Mr. Prothero, "all this talk—how can you waste so much time—if it's really as serious as this? Why don't you just ring up and say that nobody's to leave the Cherry Orchard until tomorrow night?"

They turned to him then, grinning broadly, as if, thought Mr. Prothero irascibly, he'd said something positively absurd.

"We can scarcely do that," Hugh said.

"But, damn it, you'll have to do something," exploded Mr. Prothero. "You can't just let them all be killed by a road hog from Birmingham off with another man's wife."

"It isn't—just a question of being killed," Giles said slowly. "It's crippling injuries, unnecessary suffering that we're up against here—"

"We're not always snooping round people, and interfering with their plans, you know, Mr. Prothero," said Hugh. "Just now and then, in the meshwork of their lives, comes a point like this, at which we must try to intervene."

"Well, then, why don't you get on and do it?" snapped Mr. Prothero.

"It isn't quite as simple as that," said Laura, tucking a friendly hand under Mr. Prothero's arm. "You see, the Charter explicitly forbids us to interfere beyond the limits of any living being's free will. Morality has nothing to do with these limits. Conventions haven't any importance at all. The motive is always the reality and the act only its following shadow. So—"

"You trying to tell me you can't help them?"

"No. We most certainly can. If they'll let us."

"But surely you can get one of them to listen?"

"Mebbe," said James Grant. "But we can't force it. It wouldn't do, ye see. We're not omniscient. But even if we were, how could we take a liberty that the Lord himself won't take?"

Mr. Prothero bit his lip as he swung back towards Laura. This free will—the inexorable logic of it—the awful courtesy of respecting a man's freedom even at the cost of his life—

"But it's—it's Andrew and Mary—my son and daughter. And Michael, he's just a baby. If you know about this—you must know how to stop it too. I'll go to the place myself. What does it matter if that sot runs me down? I can wait for them all day—"

"Wouldn't do a bit of good, Mr. Prothero," Giles said gruffly. Then, as something occurred to him, he murmured: "At least, not unless..."

"But—but whatever's going to happen to them all?" cried Mr. Prothero, appalled by the girl's grave face.

"We don't know yet, Mr. Prothero," Laura said.

CHAPTER 8

Mary opened her eyes and wondered what was going to be so nice about the coming day. It was still early, but the sun was rising and outside the window she could see the mist gently lifting from the horizon, where the pinewoods broke the sheer line of the far hills. When the mist lifted from the Forest like that it usually meant heat. And that was a mercy, because it was Michael's birthday and last night Ted had said they might all pack into the car with bathing things and make a day of it. And because nobody could decide whether it would be nicer to picnic in the New Forest or by the sea, Ted, as usual, had neatly solved the problem by deciding that they should drive out to the Forest for lunch and go on to the coast for tea.

Trust Ted to get things organized, Mary thought, looking at him with a smile as he lay relaxed beside her. Odd, he seemed almost the same age as Michael when he was asleep. What a queer thing sleep was. What happened in it? Where did one go? Why couldn't she always remember her dreams? Last night's had already vanished, but she had a feeling that they'd been important, that people had been talking about something that mattered a lot. She'd been dreaming about... about Laura again, Laura who had been her greatest friend, of whom she so often found herself thinking unexpectedly, without any apparent association, who was even now so continually, so vividly present in her dreams. There had been something, last night, for instance, that Laura had tried hard to tell her. She'd been stupid about it. It had been important, too. If only she...

The thread of thought broke off at the sound of an opening door at the far end of the corridor. Andrew, of course. Andrew going down early to feed the animals, to help old Barnes the cowman with the milking, for now they'd got quite a herd. How good Andrew had turned out to be at farm management. It was queer to think that time could glide so fast when you were happy. Why, this was actually her baby's eighth birthday, and Andrew had been with them—could it be possible—for six whole years.

Jane Oliver

Good years for them all, too. From the first it had been evident that Michael and Andrew were going to be tremendous friends, that they were completely absorbed and happy when they were together, whether they were building sand castles while Michael was still tiny, looking after the animals, or, as time passed, riding across the Forest, Andrew on the sobered, elderly Pepper and Michael on a stout black pony, with the dogs, Hamish and Scrubby, toiling at their heels.

It must have been wonderful for Michael to find anybody who entered so deeply into his world as Andrew, who had perhaps never left it, or else had thankfully taken refuge among its blessed simplicities on his return. It was good for Andrew, too. He was so happy at the Cherry Orchard that he never cared to leave it. And if all went well he need never leave it now. Ted was delighted with Andrew's work, though incapable of understanding for an instant the grave, almost religious passion with which he did it. He only knew that he had acquired a crazily hard-working manager who got more work out of the men than he'd have thought possible, and under whose supervision the whole place prospered to his complete satisfaction.

So he had gladly confirmed Andrew in his appointment, and planned later to make him a partner. It had the makings of a really good arrangement, since Ted was so often away and was glad to know that Mary need no longer be on her own when his ship was ordered into foreign waters. Andrew took his responsibility very seriously, spending hours poring over catalogues, pricing the newest implements, reading the agricultural journals, attending market and learning from the slow-spoken, shrewd Hampshire farmers something of the lore of centuries that awakened in him a sensation which was almost like memory and ran like a spring tide in his blood.

And Mrs. Prothero, who occasionally left her committees to visit the Cherry Orchard, or required Andrew to lunch with her at the Grange, was both relieved and gratified. There had been Hampshire landowners in her husband's family for centuries. How very fortunate that it was coming out in Andrew now.

But it was not the owning of land that interested Andrew, thought Mary, smiling as headlong sounds from the bedroom next her own indicated that a small boy was bouncing out of bed and hurling on his clothes, passionately making up time for having slightly overslept. It wasn't the owning of land, but the working of it, the feel of the good rich earth as he crumbled it between his fingers, learning the different textures of it, the varied ways of it and the treatment to which it would most generously respond. As Andrew groped after the technique of ploughing and dunging and resting and wheedling land to give its utmost in spite of frost or drought or tempest, his ears were alert for the note of the wind, the increasing whisper of ripening grain.

It had helped Michael tremendously with his lessons, of course. He had seen more sense in being coached by the village schoolmaster, retired since the war, now that he wanted to be able to add up columns of figures as fast as Andrew, wanted to learn to read to be able to spell out the captions under the pictures of prize stock in Andrew's magazines, to write in order to keep his own tottery entries about the profits and expenses of his hens.

But now Michael was going to school. Not far, as yet, only to the Grammar School in Ringsey, from which he could cycle home in time to give a hand with the evening jobs. And there would be week-ends and half-holidays on Wednesdays, so that he could meet Andrew in time to see something of the stock offered for auction at Ringsey market. So it wasn't a tragedy. Not really. But Mary knew that Michael had been pretty wretched that evening when his father had told him about Ringsey Grammar School, away back at the beginning of this very leave.

"After all, darling," she'd pointed out, "there's always Andrew to carry on when you're away and simply delighted to have you back."

"Yes, of course," Michael had said at once. But he'd stood there between his parents, thinking that book learning was a waste of time for a man whose whole heart was given to the land. He could read, couldn't he? And write? And add up figures now?

"You see, Mike," she'd gone on, "farming nowadays isn't what it was. There are such a lot of new things that you have to know about, things that mean maths and science as well as common sense. If you go on and take a degree in agriculture, for instance, you're going to be far better qualified to run quite a big farm than you'd ever be otherwise, the way things are now."

"Seems to me old Mr. Wood down the road gets on pretty well with just common sense," Michael had said, ruffling up his shock of hair and looking from his father, who had given his decree and was now lighting his pipe, to his mother, who seemed more inclined to talk things out. He stood there, square and sturdy as ever, in khaki shirt and shorts, his troubled face tanned several shades darker than his untidy hair.

"Mr. Wood's been at his job for half a century," said Mary patiently. "He knows it back to front. It's the job that's changing. All this modern stuff's going to make a difference, you'll have to know something about fertilizers and mechanization and all the rest of it...."

"'Tisn't the way to treat the land," Andrew grumbled from the armchair in the corner where he was reading a farming journal. "You can't squeeze extra profits out of it without paying for it later unless you play fair and put them back. There's nothing wrong with a bit of extra knowledge, though, old chap. I'd get it while you can. Never know when it'll come in handy."

Michael sighed, his hands clenched in his pockets, scuffing at the carpet with heavy shoes, desperately trying to put into words the deep instinct that went far beyond his means of expression. "Don't think I want to be educated. It isn't what I need, somehow. I just want to ... stay on here as long as ever I can."

"But you see," Mary said, "you can't tell what's going to be needed. Things are changing all the time. You may want new qualifications, so that you can take the new opportunities."

Ted took his pipe from his mouth. "I agree with your mother, old man. So that's rather that, I'm afraid."

"All right, Dad," Michael said sadly. His face was grim with the determination to show no quiver of weakness; he ducked his head and examined the knuckles of his clenched fist.

"Maths are always useful, even on a farm," Mary said. "I get quite tired of going over your poultry accounts because you've lost five shillings. If you're going to school in Ringsey you'll need a bicycle. How'd you like one from us next birthday?"

"Thanks most awfully, Mum," said Michael. But he had sounded less enthusiastic than polite. Mary had pretended not to notice, and sent Ted off to choose the finest bicycle they could buy. And now it was his birthday, and he was up already, starting in on the farm jobs with Andrew while she lay in bed instead of getting up and dealing with the preparations for what looked like being a lovely day. There was lunch and tea to pack... Mrs. Burns and young Bertha could turn out the long room while they were away... had she time to cycle to Ringsey and get some things? There was Mother to be rung up and invited to the picnic instead of just to the birthday tea... food for five for two meals.... Oh dear, what an undertaking! Was it really such a good idea after all?

Mary was surprised to find herself actually wishing they hadn't arranged to go out in the car. They could have bathed in the river and ridden in the Forest and had tea in the orchard as they'd first planned. It would have been so much easier. And it was going to be most frightfully hot. The flies in the Forest would be appalling at a picnic....

But there she checked herself and got up. "I must be getting old," she told herself. "Fancy trying to find excuses to save myself trouble by staying at home on Michael's birthday—even though he's really far happier on the farm than anywhere else. And it's the last day of Ted's leave, and the picnic was his idea. Come along now, pull yourself together, my girl."

And yet, her determination was shaken again at breakfast time, when Michael, beaming in the midst of a clutter of brown paper wrappings, with his bicycle gleaming and glinting behind him against the mantelpiece, put down his spoon to say, "Andrew, I'd quite forgotten. It's market day."

"We're not sending anything, though," said Andrew. "The calves aren't up to standard yet. Our pigs are all going to be fattened for killing. You haven't even any pullets—"

"No, of course... that's true," Michael agreed. "I just suddenly thought... I'd like to take the bike out for a spin...." He glanced at his father, who grinned, but shook his head.

"Plenty of time for that, old chap. You'll be using it every day in another six weeks or so. Holidays are getting on. Better take the chance of a trip to the sea."

"The sea...yes, of course. Gosh, that's fine," Michael said, his enthusiasm shifting at once.

"You're sure you'd really like that?" asked Mary. "It's your birthday, after all. If you and Andrew would rather bike over to Ringsey instead of coming with us, well, of course you can."

"I don't think so...it was just a funny idea," said Michael in a surprised voice. "Don't know what gave me it suddenly. Dad's leave's up tomorrow. So let's have that picnic today."

"Well, that settles it," Mary said.

But she put her hand to her brow in an odd, bewildered way. It must be thundery, she thought. She felt leaden with oppression and there was a sort of drumming noise in her head. Sometimes that meant she was going to have a migraine. "Not today, please," she found herself privately pleading. "It's Michael's birthday. I must be all right today." All the same, she'd better be careful for an hour or two. If Mrs. Burns would put on the eggs to hard-boil and start the sandwiches she might get Ted to run her into Ringsey for the extras and the ginger beer instead of bicycling. "Would you mind, darling," she said, "just running me into Ringsey in the car? You'll be getting her out soon anyway, won't you?"

"Just going to get her out now," said Ted, as he pushed back his chair. "Be ready for you outside the garage in two minutes."

But in two minutes he was back to say that both back tires were flat.

"Oh, Ted, what a perfectly frightful nuisance," Mary said. "Why don't we call the trip off and let the garage send out and do it? We can walk up on to the Forest with lunch and bathe in the river instead."

But Ted had already stripped off his coat. "Can't let a little thing like that do us down, darling. I'll get Andrew and Mike to give me a hand. I've got a couple of spares and inner tubes stowed away, as it happens."

"Well, then," said Mary, "I suppose I might as well go and give Mrs. Burns a hand with the lunch."

"Just as well, darling," Ted gave her an absent-minded kiss, then rooted in the pocket of his discarded coat for tobacco and pipe. "Easy does it, you'll find. We'll get the party launched yet, just you see." He set off, whistling, in search of Andrew and Michael, while Mary stood in the middle of the long room and wondered if she were going to be ill. She kept fancying things, like voices, kept thinking of people like Laura Ward and that boy that Joanna was going to marry, Hugh something or other, the boy who had the accident. It must be the heat or something; she was really getting quite silly. She could almost have sworn that she heard her father coming in at the garden door, but when she jumped round, of course there was nobody there. Only the massed ramblers over the porch quivered a little as if somebody had brushed past. Mary gave herself a shake and set off for the kitchen. Whatever happened she mustn't have a migraine and spoil that poor child's birthday. Perhaps if she took some aspirin and soda-mint....

In the special recording room they were watching the graph again. The red, blue, green and crimson lines which represented the household at the Cherry Orchard were tremulously stationary, while the yellow and the garish pink streaks had begun definitely to converge towards their meeting-place. Mr. Prothero noticed that the others were looking graver, and that their faces showed traces of fatigue. Sweat shone on Giles's forehead. Once he had to brush it out of his eyes. Laura seemed flushed and James Grant looked grim, and the freckles almost seemed to stand out from Hugh's white face.

"She's in the train," he said. "I tried to get one of the people in her area to work up a row with her husband over breakfast. But he got a letter that sent him to the office without finishing his second cup of tea. Then she nearly missed the train because her clocks were slow, but the other side worked in a taxi driver who just got her there on time."

"The other side?" asked Mr. Prothero.

"Oh, yes, Mr. Prothero, we don't have things all our own way," Laura said. "It's no use pretending that the forces of evil are either stupid or feeble. They're parasitical, of course, not interdependent, and they only want to batten on the people we're trying to help. But a major crisis can be like a gigantic tug-of-war."

"Look here, Laura," Hugh interrupted. "Can't you really get Michael off on that new bicycle?"

"I've tried awfully hard," Laura said wearily. "But he doesn't like to suggest it again because his father's so set on taking them out in the car."

"Mary's not usually so difficult."

"I'm afraid I can't do anything with Mary. I've spoken as loud as I dare, but she just can't catch it. And now she's got a headache. She really is feeling pretty queer. I thought she was going to see you once, Mr. Prothero, when you came in at the garden door—"

"I? I've never left this room!" said Mr. Prothero.

"But your thoughts did," James Grant explained.

"Yes, but I can't go with them!"

"Can ye not, then?" wondered James Grant.

"Heavens above, am I in Bedlam?" groaned Mr. Prothero. "Why don't one of you chattering children just go out and send them a wire?"

They grinned wryly at him, but nobody moved.

"I thought he might call it a day when he saw those tires," said Giles gloomily. "But there isn't a hope. He's got the other two sweating over them now."

"And yon's your wife, Mr. Prothero," said James Grant, "just walking over from the Grange." He pointed to a brownish streak which was moving towards the other four. "Eh, but it's vexing to see how much she misses the excitement, ever since the War ended. Poor body, she's come to set such store by it that she'll never be happy with a quiet life."

"My chap's at Basingstoke, meeting the train..." fussed Pinkerton.

"Ted's got the tires on..." said Giles gloomily.

"Mary's bringing out the lunch..."

"Mrs. Prothero's at the gate..."

The five colored streaks, all together now, began to move slowly forward, while the yellow and pink lines, side by side, slid inexorably nearer... nearer still.

"God help them," whispered Mr. Prothero, almost without noticing what words he used.

The preparations for the picnic went inexorably on, for Mary, who now had a horror of the whole thing, could not think of one sane reason for calling the car trip off. So the party packed itself into the car with lunch-baskets and bathing towels piled about them and the dogs scrambling over their knees while Michael, rather sad and silent, his mind still on his neglected bicycle, trod apologetically on their feet. Mrs. Prothero, sitting beside Ted, sympathized volubly over the trouble with the flat tires, and Mary listened to her throaty voice with a sort of desperate resignation. Her headache was so bad that she seemed to be moving through a dream.

"Dear me, such a pity. That must have given you a lot of work. And of course we're at least half an hour late in starting. I know, for you told me to be here at half-past eleven and I looked at my watch as I came in at the gate. Punctual to the minute, I was..."

"Don't you worry, Mother, I'll soon have us back on schedule again. Just a matter of keeping the foot down till we catch up with ourselves, you know," said Ted.

And Mary, sitting in the back, with Andrew and Michael and the dogs, heard unexpected words rolling at her in wave after echoing wave, so that she seemed to be hearing them over and over again. If only...if only she...could...understand...

"Well, dear, what a lovely party this is," said Mrs. Prothero, turning round to beam at her son, daughter and grandson, "all setting out with the least possible exertion, on what promises to be a most successful day. Mary dear, you're not looking nearly as well as usual, I must say. Quite pale, you are, now I get the chance of looking at you. What's the matter?"

"Nothing, Mother, honestly," Mary said. "I'm perfectly all right."

"Been doing too much, I expect. I know you young people. No stamina and no idea where to stop. Have you got a headache?"

"Not a bit, thank you," said Mary falsely. "Look, Mother, we're in the Forest now."

"Thank you, dear, but I've lived in the New Forest for about twice as long as you have, so I ought to know when we're in it and when we're not. Perhaps you've got a cold coming on."

"Mother, for pity's sake, I'm perfectly well," Mary protested, feeling her self-control slipping further from her with each probe.

"I expect you've been eating too many strawberries. They never did agree with you when you were little—gracious me, Michael, can't you control that dog of yours? He's just licked my face! Disgusting! Goodness knows where his nose has been—ugh—where's my handkerchief?" And Mrs. Prothero, effectively distracted, began to rummage in her handbag, while Michael, grinning broadly, gave his dog an unobtrusive pat.

After that there was peace for a time, while the speed of the powerful old touring car's progress blew their hair back from their faces, except in the case of Mrs. Prothero, who had looked out an old, once extremely fashionable and now rather odd-looking motoring hat with a veil which tied under her chin.

"Thank goodness I had my hair shingled," cried Mary, beginning to feel slightly better. "It's wonderful when the wind gets at it like this—"

"What it looks like," said Mrs. Prothero, withdrawing into the shelter of her veil as the car gathered speed, "is unfortunately another matter, my dear. How beautiful it is up on this ridge, isn't it? Ted, where are we going to have lunch?"

"Under that group of oaks on the sky line, I thought," said Ted, looking at his watch. "We're still just a shade behind schedule, but I rather think we can reckon to make that up between lunch and tea. So we'll just carry on till we reach the old objective. Lunch at one-thirty, do a bit of work aloft in those oaks to shake down Michael's lunch, push on again at three and we ought to make port just on four. Reckon an hour for bathing and half an hour for tea. Return..."

"Ted, for pity's sake! This is a birthday party, not a page of Bradshaw," shrieked Mary from the back.

"Sorry, sorry," chuckled Ted. "Never can get used to the way women dislike schedules. Part of the fun."

"I quite agree with you, my dear boy," said Mrs. Prothero with enthusiasm. "Cutting down a couple of minutes here and another five minutes there so that you've just time to fit in something else as well, that's my hobby, you know. What I feel is, we've only got one life and a short one at that. So we might as well fill it. And—"

Michael grinned at his mother, and Hamish, who had caught sight of half a dozen rabbits, squirmed and squealed on his knee, and Michael urged him to further efforts till Mrs. Prothero could scarcely hear her own banalities. But Andrew sat in a sort of daze on the other side of Mary, gripping the indignant Scrubby's forelegs so that he could not take the flying leap from the car he had in mind. Nothing seemed very real to Andrew today: he would scarcely have been surprised if he had suddenly been able to see through things. The long slopes of the New Forest, vivid with heather or darkly green with gorse, fled past on either side of the uneven ribbon of road along which Ted inexorably goaded the car. Now and then they passed by the side of symmetrical, fenced enclosures of oak or beech or evergreen; among their shadows the bracken was shoulder high and a few late foxgloves tapered between the tree trunks. Rabbits scuttered continually, and once they caught an exquisite glimpse of the russet coat and white rump of a running deer.

But Andrew felt as if he were looking at things through the wrong end of a telescope, so that for some reason the silly, pleasant business of the picnic was so remote as to be entirely without significance by comparison with the elements of another order of reality which battled about them, and of which he was muzzily aware. His head was not actually aching, but it felt full of noises which seemed sometimes like the roars and shrieks of an untuned wireless set and sometimes like half-heard words.

When they got out Michael said: "I should like to make a bonfire." And he set about his preparations, though nobody'd seemed to hear. It was always his way of comforting himself when things were going wrong. As far back as he could remember he had loved the apricot beauty of flames, bursting like flowers from a pile of dry wood. The sight of them always made him instantly happy again; though he didn't know why. So now, when something had so obviously begun to go wrong with his birthday treat, his one idea was to take comfort in the incomprehensible beauty of fire. He began to gather sticks in a hopeful way, piling them skillfully to allow the passage of air, and not too near the picnic party for them to start making a fuss about the smoke.

"Could you let me have a match, please, Dad?"

"What for?" Ted asked uncomprehendingly. "A fire? My good chap, you aren't allowed to light fires on the Forest. Come on now, forget it. I bet there's a wonderful lunch. Here you are. Hang on to that ginger beer."

Michael took the ginger beer. But he sighed. At lunch it was only necessary to eat a great deal and not to talk very much, for once Mrs. Prothero had a glass of cider she took entire charge of the conversation. She told a number of stories, reduced everyone to a sort of suffering coma, and was ultimately interrupted by Ted, who had forgotten about the projected tree-climbing and fallen asleep for long enough to put the schedule wrong again, since it was already after three o'clock.

"All aboard, there! We're ten minutes behind schedule now."

"Darling," said Mary impetuously, "it can't matter. It's so lovely here, with just enough wind to keep the flies off. Don't let's go on. Please, oh, please let's stay here! Who cares if we don't reach the sea?"

The urgency of her appeal surprised Ted. It even surprised herself, but the weight of foreboding was heavy on her again.

"You know me, darling," said Ted, picking up the lightened lunch-baskets and stowing them methodically into the car. "What I set out to do gets done."

Mary had a sudden impulse to refuse to move, to cling to the trunk of a great tree, to grapple herself to the very earth. If they stayed there they would be safe. If only it didn't sound so crazy to insist that they should stay.

When Laura returned to the special recording room her face was drawn with weariness, and Giles, arriving just after her, looked grey with fatigue. On the screen the two groups of colored lines were at right angles, with barely a finger's breadth between.

Ted stopped to pick up Mary, carried her across the heather and dropped her into the car. "You'll be glad I hustled, darling," he said, "when we reach the sea. Think of that bathe in cool green water. Dash it, I promised the kid his swim. You all right, Mother? Fine." He slammed the door. "All in behind? Off we go, then. Right away..."

They swooped along the open road which ran parallel with the summit of the moor, then left it for another that led between enclosures of evergreens, slightly downhill, towards the sea. Mrs. Prothero had become drowsily silent, Mary had shut her eyes and was forbidding herself even to think of being sick, Michael had ducked his head towards Hamish's wiry black coat and was telling him they'd arrive any moment now. Only Andrew was attentive as he sat there, quivering, staring at the road before him with eyes that seemed to see nothing at all.

A few yards ahead the enclosures on either side of them ended, and the road itself turned sharply to the right just as another road, concealed by the dense evergreen of the enclosure, came in to make a T junction, from the left. As they swooped towards it Ted turned half over his shoulder to shout gaily:

"Hallo, back there! Everybody asleep? How're we doing? What's the time?"

Stiffly Andrew moved his arm to look at his wrist watch, and began to answer mechanically: "Just on half-past three—" Then, in a single convulsion he struggled to his feet. Gripping the back of Ted's seat with one hand, he pointed with the other, shouting:

"Look...look there...don't you see him...right in the middle of the road...! Stop, Ted, I tell you! For God's sake, man, stop!"

Almost in the same instant Ted, responding automatically to the sudden voice of command, rammed on his brakes and the big tourer lurched and skidded to a standstill, tires screaming against the road, just as a long, low racing car driven at a tremendous rate swept across so close to their bonnet that they seemed positively to rock in the wake of its snarling speed.

"Well..." said Ted. And again, in the dead silence, "Well... of all the road-hogging bastards! Anybody see his number? I'll report him. I'll——" Then he drove across the road junction, drew up and turned slowly in his seat. "I'm frightfully sorry, everybody," he said more quietly. "And much obliged for the shout, old chap. It was pretty good work."

But Andrew still stood there uncertainly, staring ahead. He was shaking and his face was so bloodless that it looked ghastly. Ted spoke soothingly, as he would have spoken to a scared child.

"Yes, pretty good work. Take it easy, though. Take it easy now. It's all over. But just as a matter of interest, Andrew, how did you guess that car was there?"

Andrew's eyes remained blank as if he were trying to recapture the outlines of a vanishing dream. But it was too difficult. He sighed, shook his head helplessly, and sat down.

"I... I haven't the faintest idea," he said.

CHAPTER 9

Mr. Prothero put one shaking hand to his head and groped vaguely with the other towards a chair. "I—I feel so...tired," he said in a whispering, astonished voice. Then his legs sagged beneath him, and he was only just aware of James Grant's sustaining strength as he crumpled into his arms.

"Ye did fine, Mr. Prothero. Just take it easy. Take it easy, man..." James said. "Leave everything to us for a wee while..."

Jane Oliver

Mr. Prothero did not remember at all clearly what happened to him next. He had no precise memory of either eating or going to sleep, but as consciousness slowly flooded back again he was aware that in some way his strength had been restored and his body fed. For his fatigue had gone and instead of feeling faint to the point of extinction, he was vigorous, even exuberant again.

But his surroundings were unfamiliar. He raised his head and looked round with interest. He was, it seemed, lying on a plinth in another large room where the general lighting was so subdued that it was only as he became accustomed to the mellow twilight that he realized that many other plinths like his own were ranked along the walls. On them other figures lay relaxed as he had been, some of them apparently sleeping in the warm shadows, some wearing dark glasses as they lay naked under cones of colored light from powerful lamps of a pattern which was new to him. Such lamps hung over each plinth, and as Mr. Prothero raised himself on one elbow he became aware of many contrasting beams which gave an effect of surrounding rainbows, for in many cases several colors were being used, either together or in a series, so that the intervening shadows swam with every tone from crimson to rose, with every degree of green, amethyst, blue, golden, or sheer flame.

"'Ow's that now, sir?" asked a squat, powerfully built young man with a cockney twang, who looked like a prizefighter with a sense of humor. His white coat reminded Mr. Prothero of the Turkish baths to which he had sometimes gone in the busy London days when he had been working in the operating theater till he was deadbeat and hadn't the time to go to bed. "Turn over, and I'll give you a bit of a rub," the young man went on.

Obediently Mr. Prothero turned over. He certainly had been tired. So now it seemed quite natural to be lying there with only a rough towel draped over him and these skilful hands beating and kneading the muscles of his back and limbs into the sort of vigor he had scarcely imagined, till his whole body seemed so light, so supple that he found himself absurdly contemplating the possibility of birdlike, unaided flight.

"Feel a bit more like yourself, don't you, sir?" the masseur said.

Mr. Prothero sat up, letting the bath towel slide from his chest and shoulders, already bronzed from the effect of light which must have been playing on him while he slept. He was amazed by the sense of well-being which flooded through him: he wanted to leap and shout. Making a definite effort of restraint, he merely smiled.

"It's remarkable," he said. "Most remarkable. You're on to something that's new to me here," he added, nodding up at the extinguished lights.

The sturdy masseur nodded back. "Take it from me, sir, we can do quite a bit with light in this department. People 'aven't done more than begin to get the 'ang of its possibilities in the way of 'ealing and nourishment. Not on the other side of the Border. Now 'ere—"

"Nourishment?" said Mr. Prothero sharply.

"Well, take yourself," said the burly young man. "Don't actually feel 'ungry, do you? Not now?"

"I feel," admitted Mr. Prothero, "very much as if I'd had an excellent meal. Of course there are a number of ways of nourishing the tissues besides the obvious one. But—light—"

"That's right, sir. No more and no less. Call it a question of climate," the masseur went on. "In England you like your bacon and eggs for breakfast. Across the Channel it's coffee and rolls. Suits you all right once you're there, doesn't it? That's the way it is over 'ere. Just a different way of doing things again. Call it the climate, I say. Or something in the light itself, maybe. I dunno. That's just the way it is. Course, if you wants your regular sit-down meals you can try askin' for 'em. Nobody's fussy. Not 'ere. So there ain't no ruling against it. We likes to let newcomers down as easy as possible. But 'Sure you really wants 'em?' they asks. And you find you don't. Not 'ere."

"Well," said Mr. Prothero, "I suppose there's really no limit to the possibilities of further research. I've always liked to keep an open mind..." He stood up, the towel girt round him, and reached for his clothes.

"That's right, sir. Me too. I studies a bit in my spare time, see? So I come to that conclusion a good while ago. Can't 'elp it, not 'ere. Never know wot they'll show you next. Good as a play. Course I bin 'ere quite a bit now. Used to come over as a part-timer, earlier on. Working my passage, as you might say, while I was still at the Boston Street Baths—"

"Thought I'd seen you there," said Mr. Prothero.

"That's right, sir. Same old place. Gloomy, too, it was, after bein' 'ere. This work's wot I'd always dreamed of, some'ow. Scientific, and a chance of learning wot's at the back of things, too. Gives you a bit of 'ope, a lift out of the rut. You know. And of course, now I'm 'ere whole-time—" He made a sweeping gesture, suggestive of endless possibilities, his broad face puckered into a cheerful grin.

Mr. Prothero thoughtfully knotted his tie. "No limit to the possibilities? I wonder? Well, I enjoyed that. Where will the others be? Did they say?"

"Gentleman that brought you told me to say they'd be in the students' rest room," said the masseur. "You can't miss it, it's at the far end of this corridor. They're expecting you."

"Right. I'll go straight along," said Mr. Prothero. Then he hesitated. "Er—about this treatment—what happens about the fee?" He began to look through his pockets for his wallet, but the masseur, grinning broadly, shook his head.

"Money? Don't use it 'ere, sir."

"You mean the treatment's free? Well, it's a magnificent scheme—most progressive—but still—something for you—just between ourselves—"

"You can stop 'unting for that wallet, sir, thanking you all the same," said the masseur. "I'm 'ere on the same basis

Jane Oliver

as the rest," he added proudly. "No cash passes. I likes the work, same as the others. Wot I 'ave, I'm 'appy to give. Free."

He gave Mr. Prothero a little bow, then stood back, hands on hips, feet planted slightly apart, every line of his body eloquent of cheerful independence, an attitude which Mr. Prothero found almost unbelievable after a lifetime's exasperation at a series of outstretched, expectant palms, though he felt at a loss for a little, deprived of the familiar expedient of largesse. Then he held out his own hand and the masseur's big paw engulfed it.

"Thank—you, sir," Mr. Prothero said.

Following the directions he had been given, he then set off briskly down the corridor, surprised to find himself humming a polka tune to which he had danced in his youth. He realized that it would not take much to make him whistle, as he passed under an archway at the end of the corridor into the rest room, where three of the four walls lay open to the garden, which fell away in sweep after sweep of terraced lawns, set about with a few great trees.

In the rest room a number of men and women were reading. Others seemed to be asleep, while others were going in and out across the sills of the long windows which were folded right back to the corners of the walls. Others again were grouped under the trees on the wide lawns, the colors of the girls' light frocks vivid against the green.

Mr. Prothero crossed the big room towards the windows, and looked out at a gigantic lime tree, sweet with blossom. People were sitting there whom he recognized, and when Laura patted the empty chair beside her own he knew with a little flush of pleasure that it had been put there for him.

"He's good, isn't he, that chap?" Giles said.

"You do look better," Laura added.

"I feel it," said Mr. Prothero. "Wonderfully better. Always have maintained there's nothing like massage and a Turkish bath. But, by the way—" He hitched his chair a little nearer James Grant, and spoke in a lower tone. "There's just one thing that worried me. I couldn't find my wallet just now. Didn't matter, as it happened, because the chap wouldn't take a penny. But the thing is, can you tell me how I can have a banking arrangement made? Just for incidental expenses. Perhaps I could have a word with the manager of the bank you deal with here. Most uncomfortable, you know, to be caught like this. I expect your place would fix me up. I could give them pretty good references—"

"But there's no necessity—"

"My dear chap," said Mr. Prothero, "I very much appreciate the generosity of the hospital authorities towards their guests. Don't think it's that. But I'm thinking of emergencies—"

"Emergencies?"

"Well, dash it all, I might have to travel unexpectedly. I shall have to find somewhere to live. I may need things. I can't hope that the privileges of free board and lodging, for instance, will continue for ever."

"Why not?" said James.

"My dear fellow, how can they? I've got to have money, anyway. Otherwise, how can I get the things I want?"

"By asking for them," said James.

Mr. Prothero looked at him severely. "This is a serious matter," he said. "Money must be available for essential requirements. Take this enormous hospital, for instance, with all its departments and staff. I don't suppose you're asking me to believe that it's equipped and maintained—free?"

James ran his fingers through his sandy hair and looked apologetic. "I know it's awful hard, Mr. Prothero, but I'm asking ye to believe that very thing."

"Free?" said Mr. Prothero in a tone of stupefaction.

"Free as air. Ask the others," said James.

"That's right," Giles agreed.

"You'll have to believe him," said Hugh.

"But how can it be possible?" Mr. Prothero looked blankly round the circle of students, shocked by their apparent unconcern.

"Why shouldn't it be possible, Mr. Prothero?" Laura asked.

"Well—to begin with—how do the workers live?"

"By taking what they need and giving what they can," said James. "Nobody takes more and nobody gets less. Doesn't matter what their work is. Or their status. There's plenty of art here, Mr. Prothero, but there's no commerce. No four figure incomes. No dole. No Stock Exchange. No rackets. No advertisement. A man does his job because it's what he was born to do; and it doesn't matter whether he's a doctor or an engineer or a poet or a teacher or a musician or a cook."

"What happens if a man won't work?"

"Anybody in his senses will work if he's given the right work to do," said James. "Tuts, now, work's natural. D'ye not remember how ye fretted, Mr. Prothero, when ye had to retire?"

Again Mr. Prothero looked at him sharply. "I remember. But how did you know?"

James grinned and wrinkled his nose. "I just—knew," he said.

Mr. Prothero looked at him with an air of suspicion which was almost comical. "But surely we met for the first time when I came—here?"

"Not at all," said James cheerfully. "I've known you, Mr. Prothero, for dear knows how long."

Mr. Prothero frowned. "One of my students in the old days, maybe?"

"Aye, mebbe," said James, with a broad grin.

Mr. Prothero thought it best to change the subject.

"I keep thinking about that queer business of those cars," he said.

"Do you, Mr. Prothero?" Laura's innocent voice gave no indication that this had been obvious ever since he joined them.

"Yes." Mr. Prothero clasped his hands behind his head and frowned up at the branches overhead. "Of course the recording system is something I can only accept as a device which is technically beyond me. No doubt your confidence in it altered your attitude to the whole crisis—"

"We weren't cold-blooded, actually," Laura said. "Though I can see we might have looked it. It's difficult to explain the way we feel here, but we know that people are free, and we also know that every single one of them matters enormously. But actually it's their freedom we're chiefly concerned with at this stage, because it's something we've got to learn to respect. Their safety is in more experienced hands than ours."

Mr. Prothero considered this. "But," he said at last, "if you really take this question of free will so seriously, aren't you bound to feel that you've no right ever to intervene? How was I successful where you had been able to do nothing? Giles said intervention was impossible—"

"Except under certain conditions, Mr. Prothero," said Giles placidly. "I was going to explain what they were, but you made your own ultimate appeal first. So—"

"I made an appeal?" Mr. Prothero looked at him blankly.

"Don't you remember?" Laura said. "When it looked as if nothing on earth could prevent that crash?"

"I—appealed?"

"You prayed for them," Laura said.

"Tch, tch," said Mr. Prothero, "that wasn't a prayer. It was—er—er—pure reflex action. Only what anyone might have said. I don't suppose I meant anything by it at all—"

"Oh yes, you did, Mr. Prothero. Otherwise it wouldn't have been answered," Hugh said. "Don't ask me how it happens. I don't know. We haven't got that length yet. We're just students, same as you. One thing we do know is that it's love that works miracles, not technical skill, and that sort of heart's prayer—when there isn't time to weigh things up and consider and try to strike a bargain—that's what we call the ultimate appeal. Because of the way you felt about those people you were able to do more for them in that instant than all the scientific gadgets in creation could have done, just by crying out for help."

"I didn't," said Mr. Prothero rather crossly, "I was taken off my guard, that's all."

"Well, whether you knew what you were doing or not, your appeal was answered, Mr. Prothero," Laura said soothingly. "We'd done all that we dared. But God—"

"God?" Mr. Prothero looked quite shocked. "You mean—you actually believe in—what difference do you suppose what you call God can make?"

They looked at him thoughtfully, without surprise or disapproval; concerned only, it seemed, with the best method of explaining something which he was liable to misunderstand.

"Just the difference, Mr. Prothero, between night and morning, I think," Laura said.

"Nonsense!" said Mr. Prothero violently.

"All right. Have it your own way," Giles said. "There's no hurry about anything here."

"Here...here...here! That's the whole point. Where am I?" said Mr. Prothero with sudden desperation.

"In one of the biggest hospitals of the reception area, Mr. Prothero," said Hugh. "It's at the foot of the range of hills that they call the Edge of the Morning, and—"

Mr. Prothero held his head and groaned. Was he going mad? Ought he to ask for treatment? But as he remembered the Mental Home in which he had visited Andrew terror gripped him. Better tell nobody. At least so far he had been put under no restraint. As he reached this decision he was aware that Laura was speaking again.

"I wish you'd look in on my mother next time you're at the Cherry Orchard, Mr. Prothero," she said. "I'd be so grateful if you could cheer her up. I've tried and tried to reach her but she just thinks she's having a nightmare and screams till she wakes herself up."

"Mrs. Ward? Yes, of course I'd be pleased to have a talk with her," said Mr. Prothero. "I'll call on her the next time I'm that way. Your father took the Old Mill, didn't he—?"

"Yes," said Laura, speaking with unusual emphasis, "you'll find my mother, Mrs. Ward, at the Old Mill...."

But her words seemed to follow him from a great distance, to be drowned in an increasing roar of sound. Of course, he was crossing the bridge over the millrace at the Old Mill. No, he was shaking hands with Mrs. Ward. The first impression slid imperceptibly into the next as the roar of rushing water changed into the monotonous sound of Mrs. Ward's oddly lifeless voice. Her hand lay flabbily in his. It was cold and inert as if her blood scarcely warmed her body. Instinctively, Mr. Prothero's fingers edged round towards the pulse which seemed barely to flicker beneath them. He pursed his lips. Had Dr. Ward, he wondered, any idea of his wife's state of health?

". . . kind of you to spare the time to visit an old friend. My husband is always so busy and Joanna just moons about. I find the days very long."

She withdrew her hand. Mr. Prothero took the chair she offered him. He was sincerely disturbed by her appearance. They had told him that Mrs. Ward was unhappy, but not that she was actually ill. She looked, he thought, like someone who was dying from loss of blood. In a doctor's house, too. Could the poor chap really have noticed nothing? If he knew about her condition, what had he done?

"I'm quite well, you know," said Mrs. Ward, with the ghost of a smile. "Too well, I'm afraid. Life means nothing to me. It seems a waste, doesn't it, that I should be so well?"

"Tch, tch," said Mr. Prothero. "Never a waste to be well. Illness is the waste. Waste of time, waste of life, waste of opportunities. Life's too short, Mrs. Ward—"

"I find it too long," said Mrs. Ward. "I only want to die."

Mr. Prothero looked at her with distaste. He disliked morbidity. People couldn't live without the will for life, admittedly, but there seemed to be something futile about the desire for death. It didn't appear to achieve its objective, any more than dogged determination ever resulted in sleep. Perhaps the law of reversed effort came into play in both cases.

"But of course it doesn't matter. It doesn't matter to anybody what happens to me...."

"Surely," said Mr. Prothero, "it matters very much. To your husband. To your daughters."

"My daughters?" The words seemed to sting Mrs. Ward into sudden resentment. Blotchy, threatening color crept across her cheeks. "Haven't you heard about Laura? We've lost her," she said. There was resentment as well as grief in her voice. It creaked as discordantly as a door swinging in the wind.

"Yes. But——" began Mr. Prothero. He broke off, uncertain of what he had been going to say. He felt confused. Some morbid influence seemed to reach almost visibly towards him, threatening to overwhelm his senses in a numbing, lethal grip. He began to feel lightheaded, bewildered, heard his own voice stumbling over the fragments of what he had come to say. "Laura...doing splendidly...don't think you realize quite...nature of her opportunity..."

"It must be nice to have such comforting beliefs."

"But——" Mr. Prothero ran a finger round the inside of his collar. It must be nonsense, hysteria, but he felt as if he were suffocating. The air in the room seemed to have been replaced by something which he could scarcely breathe. His eyes were dim. His voice was beaten back into his throat. Every breath hurt his chest. He felt unreal. He couldn't remember what he'd come to say, though he still clung to the conviction that it was supremely important. He had promised someone to tell Mrs. Ward something or other. He'd expected it to be easy. But he was finding it impossible.

"Laura's perfectly all right——" He could hear his own voice battling through the obscurity that had surrounded Mrs. Ward from the moment she had first mentioned Laura's name.

"Just a beautiful hallucination," said Mrs. Ward.

Mr. Prothero struggled desperately to regain his professional calm. He was dealing with derangement of an unusual sort. It was not, he was pretty sure, caused only by grief. Grief alone, in his experience, did not derange. He could not convince her of Laura's well-being because, for some inscrutable reason, she did not wish to be convinced.

So far his failure was unexpected but comprehensible. But he was aware of more than failure: he fancied he could feel the presence of actual shapes of darkness which had taken advantage of their victim's selfish, resentful misery to batten and breed there, assured of a human host for as long as she cherished her grief, creatures who now rose like a horde of blood-sucking bats, intent on driving away the intruder who ventured to threaten their claims. Mr. Prothero drew his hand across his eyes, hunching his shoulders in a movement prompted by the almost painfully vivid impression of claws about to be hooked in his flesh. This was nonsense. Probably the air in the room was vitiated. Nobody could have opened a window for months. Lack of proper air was making him faint. That was all. Of course that was all. Everything else was sheer imagination. How could he be sitting there in a country drawing room in a part of the English countryside in which he had lived for many years, and at the same time be fighting off hordes of darkened spirits which were surging towards him, seeping through him, reaching malevolently towards the nerve centers of spine and brain? He must get out... he must get out... but not because of the forces of evil... the almost visible personifications of darkness which had fastened on this receptive soul... not because of them. He didn't believe in them... he didn't... he didn't... there was nothing hideous, miasmic in the air. But he must get out all the same. Just because Mrs. Ward didn't open her windows and he would stifle if he didn't get out....

"... kind of you to come, Mr. Prothero. I'm afraid I wasn't very good company. Life's such a mockery now. But I hope you'll come again. My husband would be delighted—"

"Of course, of course. And I hope I shall find you feeling much better—"

"Better? I hope I shall be dead."

"Tch, tch. No sense in that, you know."

"There's not much sense in anything, Mr. Prothero."

"Good-bye... good-bye..."

How absurdly difficult it was even to rise from his chair, to shake hands, to move towards the door. Mr. Prothero blundered across the dim room, feeling as if lead had been pumped into his veins, each movement a gigantic enterprise against the backward suck of an incomprehensible vortex which threatened to overwhelm the last vestiges of his will. Then, suddenly, it was over. He was in the open air again, drawing his first free breaths, hearing the roar of the millrace, blinking at the double rank of enormous oriental poppies which flanked the path to the front door.

Mr. Prothero dabbed at his forehead. He hadn't the slightest idea of what had happened. But he was aware of an overwhelming sense of relief, a relief far beyond anything he could have expected to feel after escaping from a trying and unsuccessful interview with a neurotic woman. He was puzzled by a sense of personal deliverance from evil, a conviction of actual and blessed escape. Urged only by the desire to put as much distance as possible between himself and Mrs. Ward, he hurried towards the bridge. Once across it, he would be out in the comfortingly familiar country road, and the oddly alarming business would be over at last.

But as he reached the bridge he remembered uncomfortably that Hugh had asked him to try and have a word with Joanna, who'd been scared and miserable ever since he went away. Mr. Prothero walked more slowly: he could not cross the bridge without passing her, for she was actually standing on it, leaning on the rail as if the tumult of the churning water drew her like a charm. He looked warily at Joanna, for he doubted if he could endure another interview like the last. But Joanna was different. She looked wispy and pathetic, but there was nothing actually alarming about her. She was forlorn as a lost lamb. Mr. Prothero felt his confidence returning. She was just a silly young thing. He would be bracing but kind.

"Well, Joanna," he said briskly, "that's an odd way to spend an afternoon."

"Is it?" said Joanna vaguely. "I haven't anything special to do."

"Why not? Surely a country doctor can always do with company on his long rounds? You might be very useful to your father. You could learn to drive his car." Mr. Prothero's fingers beat an exasperated little tattoo on the rail of the rustic bridge. He remembered Joanna as a long-legged, athletic child, and did not care much for this Ophelia who hung about bridges and let her hair come down.

"Yes, I suppose I might," Joanna said. "But I just don't seem to have any energy these days."

"Why not?" asked Mr. Prothero again.

"Oh, I don't know," said Joanna in a flat voice. "My nerves have been all to bits ever since Hugh—Hugh had his accident. Seems queer to think that it's six years ago already. D'you remember Hugh, Mr. Prothero?"

"I've just been talking to him about you," Mr. Prothero said. "He asked me to tell you about his work, and to say

MORNING FOR MR. PROTHERO

that when he can get leave he wants to tell you all about it himself. He also said you were to cheer up at once," he improvised. "Hugh is perfectly all right and extremely busy. I can tell you more if you're interested," he added, ignoring her stupefied face, "since I've just come from the hospital where—"

Joanna suddenly screamed. Shuddering, she covered her face with her hands. "The hospital...the hospital...that was where they took him...."

"Nonsense," said Mr. Prothero. "He's not there as a patient. He's working there. Doing a really good job, too. Now, Joanna, for pity's sake don't carry on like that. I thought you'd be pleased."

But Joanna just rocked to and fro, shaking her head, tears trickling between the fingers that covered her face. "I'm scared," she whispered. "I couldn't bear it. Don't let him come here. I'm scared, I tell you...I can't bear to think of Hugh like a ghost in a white sheet...."

This is shock, thought Mr. Prothero. No use giving in to it. "Joanna, you're being absurd," he said. "Just because Hugh had an accident—and was taken to the hospital, I suppose—why should you behave like this?"

"Because...because I don't want to see a ghost," bawled Joanna.

"But what in the name of wonder," almost shouted Mr. Prothero, "makes you think that Hugh's a ghost?"

Joanna slowly took her hands from her face and quiveringly confronted Mr. Prothero like an infant mask of tragedy. "Be—because I—I know he is," she cried. Then, before Mr. Prothero could speak again she had dodged past him and fled up the poppied pathway, to fling herself in desperation against the heavy wood of the closed door, beating on it with violently clenched fists. As Mr. Prothero hesitated, wondering if he should follow her, the door opened and she stumbled in, clapping it frantically behind her.

"Well...I don't know," said Mr. Prothero. "I must say I don't know what went wrong...."

He debated going back, ringing the bell and insisting on seeing Joanna. But he could not bring himself to face the possibility of another encounter with Mrs. Ward. He too felt exhausted, drained, as if all the life had seeped out of his own body, to leave it a rattling shell. Perhaps he was going to collapse. But the last remnants of his will drove him on. At least he must not collapse there, not in that garden, not within reach of whatever darkness brooded and crept about Mrs. Ward. If he could only reach the Cherry Orchard he would be all right. He could rest there, rest in the sunshine on his favorite seat at the end of the rose-alley. Rest...rest...how he wanted to rest....

"Hullo, Grandfather! I say, I did hope you'd be here. Sorry to interrupt your snooze, Grandfather, but honestly, I'm in a bit of a jam. Grandfather, Grandfather? I say, you're all right, aren't you?"

Mr. Prothero slowly raised his chin from his chest. His eyes were blank at first, then they focused on Michael's anxious face, and Michael's gruff young voice, occasionally leaping an octave into falsetto, still sounded in his ears.

"Course I'm all right," said Mr. Prothero.

With a sigh of relief Michael plumped himself down on the seat beside him. He wore a school blazer and his bare knees were variously scarred. A vivid cap was pushed distractedly to the back of his fair head and his satchel was still slung on his back.

"I did hope you'd be here," Michael said. "You nearly always are, somehow, when things go wrong."

"Huh. What is it this time?"

"Everything, just about." Michael's voice was despairing. "They're going to send me away."

"Send you away? Where to?"

"To public school. Dad's set on it."

"And you're not?"

"I'd rather die," Michael said vehemently.

"Nonsense," said Mr. Prothero.

"Well—I just hate the beastly idea—"

Mr. Prothero considered the boy beside him. Queer, he no longer felt tired. He was aware of a glow of happiness as he realized that Michael had come to look for him and that, in the moment of his need, he should have been there.

"I don't know what there is about this place," Michael was saying. "I feel I can't ever have enough of it, somehow. As if—as if it's too good to be real, and it mightn't—mightn't be there when I came back."

"You can't lose places just by going away from them," said Mr. Prothero. "Look at me. I keep coming back, don't I?"

"Yes."

"Things always seem specially good, you know, after you've been away."

"Sometimes," Michael said, prodding with the heel of his shoe at the weeds that crept between the brick paving, "sometimes I feel that I'd like to dig myself into the ground like a tree."

"People," said Mr. Prothero practically, "can't go behaving like trees."

Michael gurgled with laughter. "It sounds so silly when you put it that way."

Mr. Prothero laid a hand on the boy's bare knee. "I know it wasn't silly the way you meant it, old chap. But it's a mistake, usually, to hang on to things. One doesn't keep them that way, I've found."

"You'd advise me to agree to go?"

"I'd advise you to give the thing a trial."

"All right..." Michael grinned rather ruefully. "Suppose I might as well. I'll try to...remember..." His voice grew vague, as if it came from a distance. "Got...to...be...going...now...."

Mr. Prothero was alone in the rose-alley.

At least...Uncertainty hazed his mind, as if he were awakening from a dream. No...he was back again in that far corner of the hospital grounds which was still being reclaimed from thorn and scrub. Mr. Prothero rose hurriedly. The place tended to give him the creeps. Besides he wanted company, and here he was alone, except for the man he had seen there before. The gardener, he supposed, still working his way deliberately through a thicket of thorn bushes. As Mr. Prothero passed he raised his head and looked at him as he had done before. And, as before, Mr. Prothero was aware of a sensation of violent shock. Averting his eyes he walked on, unreasonably irritated. Working among such sharp-spined stuff, why did the man not wear gloves? His hands...

On the far side of one of the lawns Mr. Prothero was tentatively accosted by a young man he had not met before, but who seemed to know him, at least by name.

"I wonder if I could have a word with you, Mr. Prothero. I'm Bill Dent, and I'm expecting to have quite a bit to do with Michael, once he goes to school."

Mr. Prothero looked with interest at the stocky young man who had fallen into step beside him. He was perhaps less forcible than Giles, but he looked as if he had more humor, and there was something strenuous, almost triumphant about him, something that suggested mortal conflicts recently endured, from which he had emerged with courage and understanding and new gentleness. He had the look of an explorer. It was only later that he discovered that he had been an airman.

"Really?" he said. "Well, I'd be glad to give you any help I can. You're one of the masters or something of the sort, I take it?"

"Something of the sort," Bill agreed.

"But—what about his parents?" asked Mr. Prothero. "Can—ought you not to go to them for your information?"

"Oh, sure. But in some ways I rather think you can help me more than either Mary or Ted. So I hoped I could come and ask your advice, too." Bill looked both anxious and friendly. It was impossible not to like him.

"Maybe we could get together now and then?"

Mr. Prothero smiled. It was easy to respond to the candor of this abrupt young man, and the thought that he was needed again always brought comfort.

"I'll be delighted, of course," he said.

CHAPTER 10

Mary had never known Ted so absolutely set on anything before, nor so voluble in a terse, explosive way. Usually he was perfectly ready to listen to her ideas and check them up against his own. But this time he just clamped his teeth on the stem of his empty pipe and said he'd made up his mind what was right for Michael and there it was. The kid's name had been down for Oundrow ever since he'd been an infant, and to Oundrow he must go. It was his own old school, it had a first-rate science side and it specialized in preparing boys for special entry into the Navy.

"But, Ted, I don't think he wants to go into the Navy. You can see for yourself that his whole heart's in the land."

"Can't help that, my dear. Must equip the boy for the sort of life he's likely to have to lead. He isn't going to be given the chance of pottering about on the land. Nor is anybody else of his age, either. You don't want him conscripted into the army at the last minute, do you?"

"No—but—"

"You've got to face facts, Mary," said Ted, jabbing his points home with his pipestem. "And there's trouble brewing beyond a shadow of doubt. If the kid gets all set for the sort of Service job that's coming at him anyway he's going to be able to make the war part of his career, not just a senseless interruption of it."

"But, Ted, you can't—know—that there's going to be war?"

"As near as makes no difference, believe me," Ted said grimly. "Don't look like that, love. When you're in the Service war isn't all that bad. It makes sense of all the routine jobs you've practiced and rehearsed and made-believe with so long. I'm quite serious, not just bloody-minded, when I say I want Michael to leave home now. Otherwise, it's going to be too damn hard for him—later on."

"But, Ted, need we spend all our lives preparing for war? If it's going to come, can't we be happy till it does? Must Michael's life be spoiled because of something that may never happen? He cares for nothing but the land.

How can it be reasonable to try and break the love he has for it—"

"Modern life isn't reasonable," said Ted. "It's mostly crazy. But it's tough, too. I want the kid to get used to that, or it's liable to hit him too hard."

"But, Ted, it's you that's being hard...."

Ted shook his head. "You've got me wrong. If there's no war by the time he's through with his schooling, I won't insist on the Navy. He can go to the university for this agricultural degree that you suggested. Then if I'm wrong he comes back with a lot of extra information and starts on this blessed farming job. And if I'm right—well, it'll have to be one of the Services anyway. How's that? Oundrow next term—"

"If you're set on it—"

"I am set on it."

"Then that's that, I'm afraid," Mary said.

"Good girl." Ted put his arm round her rigid shoulder, gave it a pat, then strolled away. But Mary felt as if she had unexpectedly found a six-foot brick wall blocking a familiar and much-loved lane. She stood in front of the rain-lashed window in the long room, drumming her fingers on her desk and watching Michael, head down over his handlebars, whirl round the corner by the garage, rain streaming from his mackintosh as he propped the bicycle against the wall and dashed off towards the yard with his satchel of books still banging on his back, shouting for Andrew to know the result of the vet's examination of an injured cow.

Could it possibly be, Mary wondered, that Ted unconsciously resented Michael's devotion to Andrew? Surely not. The boy had to be devoted to somebody, with his father so much away. And it was obviously such a healthy, simple-hearted friendship between two creatures who both loved the same things, whose feeling for the land and its age-old skills was as strong and splendid as Ted's own feeling for the sea.

But how was it that he couldn't understand that other people might not thrive on the things he lived by, might express the same loyalty in other ways? She wished it had been possible, just for once, to get Ted to see things from another point of view. She'd failed. And Michael would fail too, poor child, when he made his final desperate, clumsy appeal. But to her surprise Michael made no appeal at all. He looked as if he were about to speak, seemed to remember something that made him change his mind, and stood silent, rather flushed and breathing heavily through his nose.

"Any complaints, old chap?" Ted said.

"No." Michael's voice was gruff. But it did not falter.

Andrew said nothing when the news reached him, but his face was strained and blank, and he was not much about the house for the next few days. Mary's only glimpse of him during the crisis seemed that of a remote figure following his horses over the cloud-curdled, autumnal sky line, a scud of sea gulls at the tail of his plough.

There were many difficult days in 1931, when the whole civilized world seemed to lie in the trough of a slump. All over the country small farmers struggled against large-scale overseas rivals, great tracts became Distressed Areas and stories of hunger and want were given a sharper edge by tales that in some parts of the world prices were artificially kept up by pouring milk down the drains or dumping coffee into the sea.

By 1933 things looked even worse. Michael had been at Oundrow for nearly two years. Other people had begun to talk like Ted about the chances of another war, and when she heard them Mary's heart seemed to sink right down through her body as it did when she went down in a fast lift. And then it slowly worked its way back again as her natural serenity asserted itself. Whatever might lie ahead, her whole instinct was to deal with the present, which was her immediate concern. And so she went about the Cherry Orchard as the year began, thinking of Michael's clothes which must be mended and replaced for next term, of Andrew's socks which needed darning, of her weekly letter to Ted, now with his ship in Far Eastern waters, wondering what to say to Mrs. Burns about Bertha's ambition to be a housemaid at the Savoy, and whether she ought to invite her mother to lunch next week.

The end of the Christmas holidays was unexpectedly delayed, as it happened, by a contact with a case of scarlet fever which kept Michael exultantly at home over the icy spell at the end of January. Frost bound the countryside in lead and silver: riding was out of the question, and the farm lands were raided by hopeful groups of emaciated ponies from the Forest itself, who scudded along the roads on unshod feet, snatching at every wisp of hay available, while the cattle stood in the spangled fields half shrouded in their own breath as they chewed at the mangels spread for them.

Michael and Andrew were kept busy all day long carrying fodder and repairing fences and cow barns, stables and hen houses, or breaking ice on drinking troughs. They came in for tea at dusk with scarlet faces, talking volubly of all the things that still remained to be done.

"If only I didn't have to go back to school..." Michael said, a dozen times a day.

Andrew nodded, but made no comment. At thirty-seven, he seemed scarcely older, Mary thought, than when he came to them just after the war. He was much quieter, certainly, than he'd been in the old days, but touchingly happy, shrewd within the limits of his interests, giving Michael all the hoarded devotion of an austere life. When Mary remembered the years Andrew had spent in the Home she felt that merely to have him there with them, quiet, contented and well, was almost miraculous, almost enough. But sometimes she also remembered what her father had told her about the bridge Andrew had crossed into normality. He seemed to have remained just a few steps beyond it, without venturing further, and it made her wonder whether, if things went wrong enough, he was at all likely to retreat again. But she pushed the thought away. Andrew was happy at the Cherry Orchard when Michael was with him, but he was quietly contented even when he was there alone, as if the love of the place which they shared was in itself a link between them, so that while they both loved and dreamed of the Cherry Orchard neither could entirely be alone.

But Michael's school reports showed that he had never really settled down. His work, the masters said, was uneven, could often be better, showed ability but not application, was occasionally brilliant, but almost entirely lacked ambition or drive. He had achieved no distinction of any sort and was already thinking of the time when he would be allowed to leave.

"Then what?" Mary asked him as they sat by the log fire in the long room one evening. She looked at him shrewdly over the edge of her horn-rimmed glasses as she pushed the darning needle over and under across the heel of one of Andrew's socks.

"Back home if I thought I'd half a chance with Dad," said Michael in his newly gruff, still uncertain voice. He was sitting on the sheepskin rug in front of the fire, his wrists shooting out of the sleeves of his school sweater, a gap showing between sock and trouser leg as he clasped his hands round his knees. But Michael hadn't changed much in essentials, either, Mary thought, as she watched him. He was still the same fair, sturdy child, in spite of deep voice, long trousers and slicked hair.

"I'm afraid you haven't a chance," Mary warned him. "Your father said in his last letter that you'd better make up your mind whether it was to be Cambridge or the Navy pretty soon. So you've got a choice. He isn't being unreasonable. And Cambridge—I take it you won't choose the Navy—might come in pretty useful, too."

"Yes," Michael said. Then he threw on another log and they watched the river of sparks swirl up into the blackness of the chimney.

"And you're taking School Certificate this year. Then there's only your exam for Cambridge, and you might get exemption from that."

"Yes," Michael said.

"And you can leave with an easy mind then, can't you?"

"Oh, yes, Mum," Michael said.

Mary leaned forward and tweaked his ear as he hunched himself a little nearer the fire. "Do stop being so Byronic about it. Everybody goes to school. Most people want to go to Cambridge."

"Well, I don't," said Michael explosively. "Oh, I'm sorry, Mum, but I just don't care for it. I don't know why. I've got lots of friends—pretty good chaps, too. But—well—when you compare it with this place it—it doesn't seem real. Mind you, I wouldn't say that to anybody but you, and I expect even you think it sounds crazy."

"No," Mary said. "I know about that, too."

"Do you?" He looked at her, half hopeful, half suspicious, under his brows.

"Yes, of course. Some places do feel more real than others. I don't quite know why, or whether everybody feels that way or only just some people, like us. Some places are real in dreams, too. The Cherry Orchard is. It's just as real sleeping as waking. Realler, perhaps. Tell me, Michael—this isn't actually a change of subject—have you a friend called Bill?"

Michael shook his head emphatically.

"That's funny," Mary said. "It came into my dream that you had. I started by dreaming about your grandfather, like I often do, even now—"

"I never seem to dream anything, nowadays," Michael said. "But I used to dream like a monkey when I was a kid. All about you and Andrew and the good times we had here. Used to dream about an old chap who said he was my grandfather, too. Of course, I suppose I might have invented that, because I knew what he looked like from his photographs, but he used often to be pottering about at the far end of the rose-alley—"

"That always was his favorite seat," Mary agreed.

"Or sometimes he'd be sitting in the chimney corner in the long room," Michael said. "Not talking a lot, but enjoying himself, just being there and seeing what was going on. Kids make up a lot of tripe," he said apologetically, "but I remember quite well how I used to reckon he'd be around somewhere when I was bothered about anything. Of course I don't dream like that now. All nonsense, I suppose."

"I'm not sure," said Mary thoughtfully, "that it was. Nobody really knows what happens in sleep, Mike. Perhaps you do dream but don't remember. Anyway, last night

I dreamed that your grandfather was here again, sitting in the chimney corner, like you said, in this very room. He just came in and said 'hullo' as usual; then he asked where your father was and I said 'with his ship.' I remember he said, 'Funny. I never seem to see him, do I? even when he's on leave,' and then he settled down in his corner. You were here too, and this man called Bill. They were teasing us and laughing about the fuss over school. Bill was specially nice. I liked him more than any of the boys you've brought home. He was older, of course; sort of quiet and strong. I thought he might be one of the masters—"

Michael grinned. "Not ruddy likely, Mum, begging your pardon. Dash it, I spend most of my time dodging out of their way. What's this chap do, any way?"

Mary paused with her needle half threaded. "I know it sounds funny," she said, "but I only remember that he said he knew you very well already but you'd know him better after you'd learned to fly."

"Well, I think something you ate must have upset you, Mum," said Michael. "If you ask me, all the aviating I'm likely to do will be over a pony's head when he puts his foot in a hole."

Next day the thaw began all over England. On Monday Michael went reluctantly back to school and in Germany Adolf Hitler was elected Chancellor of the Third Reich.

It was just after Mr. Prothero had returned from one of his visits to the Cherry Orchard that he met James coming from the general recording room. He looked grave, and turned back with Mr. Prothero. "Just have a look at this," he said. Mr. Prothero went with him reluctantly. He did not care much for the phenomena of the general recording room. The walls had darkened since his last visit, he noticed, and even such light as there was showed luridly from under a clinkerlike sediment. Peering about in the sulphurous glare, Mr. Prothero could just make out Laura and Hugh in the group in front of the map of Europe.

"Where's Giles?" he asked.

"Gone to see if he can contact Ted," Hugh explained. "He hasn't been able to get anything across for quite a while. He's shut himself right off; a pity, with so much tricky stuff ahead. Just look at this, James."

He pointed to the dull smoulder in Italy, a sullen clash of sparks in Spain, a threatening heave of cruel, thunder-murky luminosity in Germany, a twilight obscurity which was creeping across France towards England, and a sinister, lava-like movement in the Far East. Mr. Prothero found himself staring helplessly, dazed by the threatening lights, vaguely aware of voices round him which seemed to come from another dimension, while his friends stood silent by his side.

There were many voices, deep and strong, yet terrible in their passionless serenity, beautiful as the voices of angels who still beheld the glory of God as they recorded, without wrath or censure, the incomprehensible follies and sorrows of man. As they spoke the years seemed to fall on the world like drops of November rain.

"The World Economic Conference has failed..."

"Japan has withdrawn from the League of Nations..."

"Germany, too, has withdrawn..."

"The Disarmament Conference has achieved nothing..."

"The British Prime Minister has refused to receive the hunger marchers..."

"The people of the Saarland have elected to return to the Reich..."

"The Italians have invaded Abyssinia..."

"The British King is dying at Sandringham..."

"The Germans have marched into the Rhineland..."

"Civil war has broken out in Spain..."

Suddenly Mr. Prothero put his hands over his ears. "I can't bear it. I can't bear any more..."

At once Laura's hand was on his arm. "Come with me. We'll get right outside for a bit, shall we?"

"Yes... yes," said Mr. Prothero. "I've got to get away."

He felt dizzy again. The sinking feeling gripped him. He thought he was going to faint, but he could still feel Laura's hand, warm and strong, within his. He clung to it as if it were his one link with reality and was presently aware that they were walking together down a tree-shadowed summer lane between a cornfield and a hazel copse in which the birds were singing.

"Better, isn't it?" Laura said.

Mr. Prothero ran agitated fingers through his hair, his trained recording faculty making him notice, even now, that he was surely less thin on top than he used to be.

Must be the climate or something. "Yes, yes, that's definitely better. It was dreadful. The future coming down on the world like an avalanche that no one knew about in time to stop. All the little people, the cannon-fodder, the obedient, the inarticulate—being shovelled into the jaws of this Moloch, this monster—"

"No," said Laura suddenly. "It isn't like that at all."

"But I've just seen it," said Mr. Prothero. "In that recording room or whatever it's called. These gathering forces, that inexorable future. No choice, no mercy, nothing to be done—"

Laura put her hand over his. "Dear Mr. Prothero, you needn't worry so," she said. "That's only one side of it. You've just seen a cosmic diagram of the results of greed and selfishness on a world-wide scale. But that's no more the whole truth about humanity than a temperature chart is a complete picture of a living man. It's true as far as it goes, that's all. But all the qualitative things have been left out. You haven't seen, as we have, the patience, the mercy, the chances offered again and again to every living soul. You've just seen freedom misused, gifts mishandled, heaven despised and God forgotten. Of course it's horrifying."

"It's heartbreaking," said Mr. Prothero.

"It's always been like this," said Laura. "In Atlantis, perhaps. In Babylon and Nineveh, Egypt and Greece and Rome. Perhaps every so often people are offered the same old choice between good and evil, and the future of their civilization depends on what their answer is."

"I shouldn't be surprised," said Mr. Prothero wearily.

"But surely," Laura said, "the important thing is that the choice is offered to us, whatever we've done, again and again and again. Isn't that part of the mercy of God?"

"I don't know," said Mr. Prothero. Abruptly he changed the subject. "Didn't I hear music just now?"

"I expect you did," Laura said. "This lane runs past one of the big song centers where all the new melodies are tried out. Anybody can go and listen. The greatest musicians from both sides of the Border meet there to hear each other's work. But I really brought you this way to see one of the training centers for people whose gifts are with crops and animals. They can come here on part-time courses while they're still on the far side of the Border, like everybody else, you know. I specially wanted you to see two people that you'll be interested in. Look, they're in the field just here."

Mr. Prothero paused at a stile which led into a gently tilted field, drowsy with evening sunshine between the high hedges that were patterned with honeysuckle and wild rose. Here and there great oaks cast their shadows far across the field. In the shade of the tall hedge a rakish little dog which seemed to be mostly Sealyham was sniffing excitedly among the tree roots, occasionally sending up a shower of earth over the baskets and cider jars beside him, while a Scottie terrier, indifferent to such distractions, sat magisterially on his master's coat.

Out in the glare a line of young men and women were gathering the swathes of hay together against the evening dew. Some of the women wore prints and sunbonnets and some were in breeches and open-necked shirts, but Mr. Prothero specially noticed a boy and girl who were working towards them. Both were tanned several shades deeper than their honey-colored hair, the girl was slight and the boy was sturdy, and their beauty reminded Mr. Prothero of the dream of Greek youth idealized on a Bacchic frieze.

"Recognize them?" Laura asked.

"I don't know the girl," said Mr. Prothero doubtfully. "But the boy—yes, of course—it's my grandson Michael. Good gracious, how he's grown. And what on earth is he doing here?"

"He's just over here on a part-time course," Laura said casually. "The girl with him is Verity. They met here some time ago, but they don't know each other yet over there. Of course they will. They're just made for each other, as the old wives say."

"I should like to speak to them," Mr. Prothero said hastily. He preferred, as usual, to ignore anything that sounded at all queer.

"Of course. I'll call them here."

Mr. Prothero expected her to speak or wave. But she just stood quietly beside him, and presently the boy and girl turned, as if at an audible summons. They came across the field towards them, hand in hand. Mr. Prothero found himself blinking as they came near, as if the sunshine had got into his eyes. It was difficult to see clearly. Now and then he fancied that only one radiant young creature was crossing the bright field towards him. But after he had given his eyes a rub things steadied, and he saw again the two young figures, sunburned and splendid, smiling at him from the far side of the stile.

"My dear boy," said Mr. Prothero, "I'm delighted to see you here. No need to ask if you're well." As he took Michael's big hand between his own he felt the vigor of the boy's young life glow up his arm, and the warmth of his greeting was an instant reassurance. No, Michael hadn't forgotten him.

"Hullo, Grandfather. It's fine to see you again. You're looking pretty good, too. Getting younger every day. Just like the old tag come true."

Mr. Prothero chuckled. "Glad to hear it. Must say I don't feel my age any more. It's being a student again that does it, I believe."

"And this is Verity," Michael said, turning to the girl at his side. "We work together here. She's going to come to the Cherry Orchard presently."

"Well, my dear, I certainly hope you do," said Mr. Prothero as he shook hands with Verity. He liked the look of the girl. No nonsense about her. Her eyes were as true as a lad's.

"I want to come to the Cherry Orchard awfully, after all Michael's told me about it," Verity said. Her voice was low, with a lilt in it, like the sound of a hill stream, Mr. Prothero found himself thinking unexpectedly. And her eyes were the same peat brown. "I'm stuck in a London job, though, at present, worse luck. I work for a firm of solicitors..." She made a little grimace. "I don't like it much. But it's near my family. My mother's an invalid, you see."

"I can imagine the work at the Cherry Orchard suiting you better than a lawyer's office," said Mr. Prothero. "But I don't suppose there's much chance of your getting away."

"There will be," said Verity simply. "I don't quite know when, but they'll tell me in time." She turned towards Michael and smiled.

"By the way, is Andrew here too?" asked Mr. Prothero.

"No," Michael said. "He won't come. I've tried hard to persuade him, but he loves the Cherry Orchard too much. He never wants to go anywhere else in case he can't get back. I understand that, you know, after what Mum told me about all he's been through."

"Yes, so can I," said Mr. Prothero gravely. Then he smiled. "You weren't so keen on leaving home yourself, in the old days, were you?"

Michael grinned. "True enough. I don't much care about it even now. But it's different when I'm coming here."

Mr. Prothero looked at him thoughtfully. "Why's that?"

Michael hesitated. "Well, I didn't like leaving the Cherry Orchard because it meant getting further from home. But this is different. I can't say more. But to come here is to get even nearer home than the Cherry Orchard is. I don't know how. I don't suppose it sounds sense."

Jane Oliver

"Well..." said Mr. Prothero.

Michael and Verity smiled at each other.

"Afraid I can't make it any clearer," Michael said.

"It's all right, Mr. Prothero," said Verity. "Lots of people feel like that about coming here. And they can't explain. Things are like that on this side. Sometimes they seem nonsense. But they still feel true. Like they do in dreams. And it's the truth that matters, surely?"

"I've always thought so. But——" Mr. Prothero broke off, aware that the intellectual boundaries of a lifetime were being assailed by unexpected ideas for whose emotional origin he had previously felt the profoundest mistrust. And yet, looking at Michael and Verity, he felt the unfamiliar faculty of imagination briefly kindle and glow. Were some aspects of truth perhaps discernible by lovers which remained hidden from less fortunate men? He screwed up his eyes because the strong light hurt them, made the outlines of the young man and woman before him waver, till they almost seemed to blend, to become one.

"We old fogies still have a lot to learn," he said.

CHAPTER 11

It was so quiet in the long room where Mary, Andrew and Michael sat beside the wireless that the noise of the match Michael struck to light his pipe seemed like a small explosion. Strange to be aware, Mary thought, in that silence, of so many million people up and down the country who were also sitting by their wireless sets, also waiting on that night of January, 1936, for news of the King. It wasn't often that one was acutely aware of all one's fellow countrymen; such awareness was always a momentous thing, born, as now, of grief; sometimes of fear or supreme joy.

Jane Oliver

She sat in her chair beside the log fire while Michael, longer legged, flashier tied, yet so much the same candid creature, prowled restlessly between wireless and fire, and Andrew pretended to do accounts at the table. And as she felt the emotion of all those other people, unseen, unknown, meet hers and blend with it, she, Mary, seemed to be no longer only one woman, sitting with her brother and her grown-up son by a Hampshire fireside, but also part of so many other women waiting by their wireless sets, in mansion and cottage, shop-parlor, lonely farmhouse, East End tenement, or suburban flat. The darning in her nervous hands might as well have been the sewing, the knitting, the embroidery, the crochet, the patching in theirs. And Michael's fingers, twiddling the knobs to make sure of missing no announcement, were akin to those of so many other sons and fathers and brothers and husbands up and down the waiting land; fingers that were gnarled or manicured, calloused, pudgy or thin, grimed or cared for, skilful in stable or counting-house, factory, garage or shop. She could hear her very voice, sharp with anxiety, asking him to leave the thing alone, go echoing through half the homes of England.

So many optimists, she guessed, must be reminding each other of the King's wonderful stamina, and the remarkable recovery he had made once before. But even as she felt their hope she also felt an increasing sense of tragedy, an awareness of change. They were awaiting not only the passing of a beloved King, but also of a whole order of existence which was ebbing with the life he had given his people. Their vigil had the solemn quality of sunset, portentous for many watchers with the knowledge that their long day, too, was indeed nearly over, and they might well be for the dark.

"The King's life," read the chief announcer, "is moving peacefully towards its close...."

In that instant Mary felt the dismay of the whole nation shake through the quiet room: it was as if a host of children, bereft of the focus of their love and veneration, had turned in consternation to each other, wordlessly asking what they should do now. It was some time before she and Andrew and Michael realized that they were all standing, as if at the national anthem. Then, embarrassed, they began looking for things, as if to explain away the instinct that had brought them to their feet.

"Turn off the wireless, Michael," Mary said.

Andrew said gruffly: "I think I'll go down to the village. I want to catch the new chap we're giving the haulage contract to before he comes out of the pub. I won't be late back."

"All right," Mary said. "I don't suppose we'll be in bed when you get in."

She picked up her darning again, and Michael, for about the sixth time, set about the business of relighting his pipe. "I'm glad he got his Jubilee."

"Yes," Mary said. "And I'm glad we were there."

"I liked the bonfire best," said Michael. "The huge one in Hyde Park that the King touched off by pressing a button in the Palace. That was terrific. I got just as near as I could."

"How you've always loved bonfires," Mary teased him. "I suppose that's why you keep on playing with that pipe. Just for the fun of getting it going again. Or because you're a Cambridge man." She was aware of being conscientiously, unsuccessfully flippant, aware too that the stress and extended consciousness of the past few hours had suddenly threatened to become more than she could bear. It was as if from that vantage point she had been able to glimpse the coming years when the whole nation, united again by danger and catastrophe, would wait by millions of wireless sets for news which only a little while ago would have seemed too hard for them to bear. She said again, "That pipe!"

Michael considered his pipe gravely. It had been a Christmas present from his grandmother. "I like the thing," he maintained. "It's just that I haven't got it properly broken in."

"It seems funny to think you'll be going back to Cambridge so soon now, doesn't it?" said Mary.

"Must say I never thought I'd get there at all," Michael said, tipping the tobacco out of his pipe on to a sheet of newspaper and scraping round the inside of the bowl with the small blade of his penknife till the noise set Mary's teeth on edge. "It certainly was tricky going last summer, when Dad was on leave. It's a funny thing: I've never known the old man so utterly un-arguable with as he's been about my blessed education, from the start to the finish. He just got hold of one idea and he's never let it drop since. Of course it's his cash and all that, and I realize he expects a say in the spending of it. But it's—well—it's my life."

Mary rooted about in her workbasket for wool to match a fresh pair of socks. So difficult, with Michael a child no longer, to be honest and yet loyal about Ted, to balance the picture Michael had made of his father with the other things that she alone knew.

"I think it's this feeling he has," she said at last, "that there's going to be a war. He's so sure that he just can't see any future for a man who doesn't make his plans accordingly. If you're in one of the Services, as he is, war's part of the program. You take it in your stride. It means quick promotion, companionship, excitement, action, steady employment, finishing up with a pension—"

"Not so sure about that. Grateful nation is liable to worship you for the duration and axe you afterwards, just when the wily ones have clamped their bottoms down on all the best jobs. Doesn't matter to me so much. It's the principle of the thing I object to."

"Well, your father's stuck to the bargain. There's no war yet, so he's let you go up to Cambridge like a lamb."

"Like a sore-headed lion, I should have said," grinned Michael. "And the thing isn't over yet," he added, beating his pockets in search of his box of matches. "He's such a persistent old sea dog, Mum, begging your pardon, that he's going back over it on every leave. Now he's with the Fleet in home waters the perennial discussion sounds like being one of those reasons why boys leave their good homes."

"Yes, I know it does," Mary said. "And it isn't a bit of use my saying that your father knows best and I won't hear a word of criticism, because that isn't going to get us anywhere. I agree with you about Cambridge. You're interested in livestock and planned agriculture. Well then, get on and learn about them. You'll get your degree, with any luck, before you have to break off—" She pulled herself up sharply, adding: "Though of course I still think there won't be any war."

Michael grinned up at her over his tobacco pouch, his forehead creased with anxiety under a strand of untidy hair. "Are you quite sure?"

"Well—" said Mary desperately. "I—I—"

"You mean you—hope there won't be any war?"

"I hope and pray that there won't be any war every single night of my life. But if there is—" She broke off, feeling again the waiting millions, aware of their tremulous hopes, their disowned fear.

"But if there is, Mum?"

"If there is, your job here will be waiting for you, your home will be behind you, our hope and love with you, whatever you do, wherever you are."

"I know, Mum," Michael said.

And he said no more. Mary wanted to hold out her arms, to cry aloud to him: "If only I could do more than just sit here and plan and argue and joke and darn for you. If only I could hold it off—this horror that's coming at us—if only I could do more...." But of course she couldn't say it, she couldn't say a single word.

"Trouble is," Michael went on at last, "I reckon Dad's certainly right in one way. It is coming—definitely. And as it gets nearer and more people start shouting about getting ready for Armageddon and all the rest of it, Dad's going to have a pretty strong case."

"I don't think so," said Mary. "He said you could go up to Cambridge, and it's only reasonable to let you finish there now."

"Perhaps," Michael said. "But there's my side to the business, too. It isn't going to be easy just to go on sitting through lectures when the world's like a stackyard on fire. Look at those Italians using mustard gas in Abyssinia and the Japs cutting the guts out of China with nobody doing a thing. There's going to be trouble in Spain in next to no time. And all we seem to be thinking of in this country is how to keep our money safe and our hands free. It's pretty complicated being young just at the moment, Mum. And it's going to get worse."

"I can see that, my dear," Mary said.

"Some chaps have gone to China. There's talk about the International Brigade. All sorts of rubbish. You know how it is."

"I know how it is," Mary said, her hands steady as she darned one of Ted's socks. "Dear knows I'd keep you in cotton wool or safe deposit if I thought any good would come of it for either of us. Knowing that it wouldn't—well—I'd just like to know what you're planning to do."

Michael got his pipe going, and took a few pulls at it before he spoke again. "Well, I worked it out this way. I don't want to go into the Navy—as a sailor. I'm quite definite about that. I don't know why. Dad talks and talks, and I know he really loves it, and that means it's just the life. For him. But not for me. I fancy flying more than the sea-dog stuff. But I think we might compromise. There's an institution at Cambridge known as a flying club, and a branch of the Navy known as the Fleet Air Arm. I know the standard's terribly high, but I can find out if I've got a chance. I can also learn to fly, while I'm still up at Cambridge. Rather expensively, I'm afraid, but I think Dad may consider it justified when I tell him what I'm after. And at the outbreak of war, well, if there is an outbreak, darling, I'll try to get taken on as a pilot in the Fleet Air Arm. How does that sound to you?"

"It sounds—it sounds all right," Mary said rather shakily. "But—what on earth gave you the idea? I didn't know you'd ever flown."

"I hadn't—before last term. It was funny the way it happened, actually. I was going off for a day's hunting with a chap from another college that I'd got to know. He'd arranged that some stables his people own would mount me, and we were to drive there in his car. But darn me if the thing didn't break down just outside the flying club. And of course I started watching. Then someone offered me a trip. It got me. Just like that. I thought of nothing for weeks except how to get into the air."

"I—see," said Mary. Her face was awed as she remembered her dream. Hadn't there been a stranger called Bill, who'd said...who'd said that Michael would know him better—after he'd learned to fly?

Michael, who so often read her thoughts, did so now, disconcertingly. "But there's still nobody around the place called Bill."

"Isn't there, dear?" said Mary casually. "Well, you haven't actually learned to fly yet, have you?"

"Not yet," Michael said, with a look in his eyes which made his mother glad that Andrew couldn't see him. "But I shall."

On the dais in the big lecture hall the man who was addressing his audience paused, seemed to gauge their mental state in a split second, then put his notes away. "I shall leave you there for the present," he said quietly. "Next time I shall take the subject up where we left off. Don't try to force your memory to grasp the details of what we have dealt with today. I shall only expect you to get hold of the broad outline of what I put before you at this first lecture. Details can always be filled in by your own widening experience. This is multidimensional stuff; it's bound to be difficult for you to retain."

Jane Oliver

He gave them a pleasant little bow and went out by the side door.

Mr. Prothero did not at once rise with the rest. The students were men and women of various ages, some jaunty still, others stunned like himself, some chattering, some silent, as they streamed out of the auditorium into the lofty passage which ran the length of the tutorial wing. Mr. Prothero had already seen something of it with James Grant when he had signed on for the course of post-graduate lectures. James had explained that everybody attended such a course of lectures when they were first posted to the hospital, and it was necessary that they should, for, as he warned Mr. Prothero, there was quite a lot that he would find new, even revolutionary, in the hospital's therapy.

And so Mr. Prothero had gone to his first lecture and found it an extremely curious, in fact, quite an unexpectedly overwhelming experience. He was still trying, as he sat thoughtfully on in his place next to the center aisle in the front row of the now empty auditorium, to get his bearings in an alarming sea of new impressions.

The director of studies had spoken himself. James said he always did at the beginning of a course. It was his duty to give his students some idea of the scope of their new environment. Mr. Prothero had been prepared to be interested, in a properly detached and scientific way, but not as youthfully enthusiastic, for instance, as James had been. He was too old a hand at the job, had heard too much of this miraculous discovery or that, and come at last to take everything he was offered with rather more than its due dose of salt.

So he had settled himself, as he had done (so long ago now) in Edinburgh as a student at the famous medical school, on one of the aisle seats in the front row where he could be sure of missing nothing, and prepared to offer the lecturer his critical attention. He was glad that things seemed to have steadied down into some sort of routine. Give him a course of lectures and he had a pretty good idea of what he was about. Much more satisfactory altogether. Took his mind off his own mental condition, which was causing him increasing anxiety. The nightmare conviction that he must be going mad had grown on him lately. If only he dared speak of it to somebody, to anybody. But... they might send him away... like Andrew, to a Mental Home... he could not bear that. The very thought brought him out in a cold sweat.

But perhaps he was exaggerating his own symptoms. Between whiles, he had to admit that he had not felt so well for half a century. On the other hand, it was disturbing to find himself completely without any sense of time, to be unable to reckon whether he'd been working at the hospital for hours or years. And those trips to the Cherry Orchard... he always remembered all that everyone said, exactly how they looked. But he hadn't the faintest idea of how he got there and still less idea of how he got back. When he was a child, of course, he used sometimes to faint in trains. Perhaps these blackouts were something like that. But did he actually faint, nowadays, on such journeys, or was he merely unable to retain any memory of them afterwards? That was what he wanted to find out. There was nothing wrong with his memory in the ordinary way.

Take these lectures, for instance; he remembered every word of them, though he had not begun to listen with any great expectations. He had meant to criticize and estimate. He had expected to be able to follow, step by step, the elucidation of the hospital's policy in regard to disease, the enumeration of new trends in treatment, the indication of the opportunities which would be offered him, both of observing other people's work and of taking up his own. Instead, he had taken part in something far more fundamental than any lecture could ever be.

He had felt himself to be literally invaded by a flood of new ideas, not merely contained by the spoken word but borne in upon him quite inexpressibly. He supposed that only one lecturer had spoken: certainly the peroration had been quietly and reasonably given by him alone. But behind him and beyond him, Mr. Prothero had been aware of a great company of people, some familiar and some strange, some half remembered and oddly compulsive, others startlingly unforeseen. Mr. Prothero screwed up his eyes and peered into the shadows behind the dais. Surely the man he had supposed to be the gardener could not also be there, in the dimly glimpsed, austere group which seemed to loom behind the lecturer?

And the lecture itself had been very strange. Eloquent as the lecturer had been, Mr. Prothero had not only heard what he had to say. He had also seen. He had been visually aware of the lecturer's conception of man, the spiritual creature; struggling, wandering, degraded, obstinately self-blinded and self-slain; tormented and tormenting, greedy and starving, vilified and debased, yet still recognizable in his pitiful state, since nothing he could ever do would quite obliterate all trace of the sublime image in which he had been made. He must still struggle, through innumerable ages of darkness of his own choosing, maimed by his own folly and the malice of his kin; groping and broken and weary of life as he had tried to live it, haunted by glimpses of life as it yet might be, turning at last to take the prodigal's path, home to the feet of God.

But he had not only seen and heard it. He had felt it all about him; the darkness and the misery and the slime. He had seemed himself to struggle up with the self-exiled race from that outer darkness and nothingness to which they had fled when once their pride-flawed nature found heaven's harmony unbearable. He had journeyed with the scattered remnants of a once angelic people through primæval ice and naked rock and fertile sludge, up from the putrid jungles and stifling swamps, encountering the first homes of creation in the nests and lairs, the burrows and holes, the warm crannies where strange, forgotten, warm-blooded mother creatures suckled the young blind things with whom love came back to the world. He had wandered on with humanity to the stifling dens, the wind-whipped caverns, the stilted lake dwellings, the beehive huts where articulate beings first stared at each other and wondered what manner of men they might be.

Beyond them lay the cottages and manors, the halls and palaces and castles, the buildings of timber and daub, stone and brick and thatch and slate and concrete and steel, the slum tenement, the luxury hotel and the service flat. There men lived and learned and fought and spent and wrangled and thought and feared and loved and worshipped, peering at last out of the limitations of their earthly existence towards something that to most of them seemed more shadowy, and to a few infinitely more real than all that had gone before.

And as they went, their hunger always drove them further; hunger that Mr. Prothero could feel twisting his own guts as the lecturer went on, hunger only for food and drink at first, but, once these were sated, hunger for other things; hunger for mating, a hunger which sometimes led on to love of beauty and sometimes to love of power; hunger for knowledge, for skill, for truth. And beyond all these again hunger still drove them on towards the nameless things of the spirit, long after the body cried for mercy, having had its fill.

Such were the longings that goaded the restless poet, the scientist, the doctor and the priest whose instinct was to minister and to heal. "To learn, that is our work here, at this hospital," the lecturer had concluded, and Mr. Prothero, as if returning from a long journey, became aware again of the lecture room, of his seat in the front row, next to the center aisle, and realized that, overwhelming as the experience had been, he had only received a mere fraction of the visible, audible and tactile impressions which he had been offered. The lecturer's final words still haunted him: "We, who have struggled with the rest of humanity through the long night of exile, stand, as every being must, sooner or later, on the edge of the morning. Our spirits are at last astir as we begin to realize the tremendous implications of that fuller consciousness, which is awareness of God."

Mr. Prothero rose reluctantly to follow the stream of students into the corridor. He had been shaken out of what he liked to consider his scientific detachment; it was a state of mind which he was never entirely to regain. For the post-graduate course was an exhaustive one, including not only lectures and demonstrations of the hospital's theory and practice in surgical, medical and psychological treatment, but spells of practical work in every department.

Mr. Prothero now encountered not merely students but their seniors, beings whom he came easily to venerate as he had venerated the professors of his far-off student days. He was able to check up their theories in the libraries of the tutorial wing; he might waylay them with searching questions which were patiently answered; in the wards he could see for himself the results of their compassionate ministry to minds diseased.

Here, thought Mr. Prothero, here at last were the answers to the questions that had anguished him all his life long. Here were people who sought the root of the matter, knew they must heal the broken heart as well as the fractured limbs. Here, in every ward and department, was the art as well as the craft of healing; the solemn and awful joy of work through the doing of which a man began to live as it had been planned that he should live from the creation of the world.

Sometimes, as he worked at his notes or followed one of the great men round the wards, stood silent in an operating theater or in the dimness of one of the ray departments, Mr. Prothero wondered when he would be allowed to operate himself. But whenever he asked questions about the probable duration of his probation he found his inquiry turned courteously aside. The length of the course varied a great deal, it depended on circumstance and opportunity, it was impossible to lay down hard and fast rules.

"You may not even find," said one of his professors, "that you wish to go on with this branch of our work. There are many others. People change their mode of expression—"

"But surely—all my experience—must it be wasted?"

"It would not be wasted. But it might take another form. We are only at the beginning of possibilities here, you know," the great man told him. "Even so, it often takes newcomers some time to grasp the great variety of their scope. Our equipment, for instance, is so far ahead of anything on the other side of the Border that most people run away with the idea that life here is highly mechanized. It isn't. It is a living, vibrant entity. No gadget cult is ever substituted for human values. All the wonders of all the worlds would swing light in the scale against the misery of one abandoned child."

"I've always believed that," said Mr. Prothero.

The professor nodded. "That belief brought you here."

CHAPTER 12

Mrs. Prothero said: "Really, Mary, I don't know what it is about you young people. I'm an old woman but I've got ten times your stamina. There you are, just wilting over that little job I gave you, the sort of thing I could have romped through at your age. You don't seem to realize we may be needed at any moment here. Any moment, I tell you, the country may have to be put on a war footing and nothing thought of, nothing done. Give those accounts to me, child. I can still add up a few columns of figures without sitting there looking the picture of misery and counting on my fingers."

"Mother, if you'd only leave me alone for thirty seconds, I'd have it done——"

"I'll leave you alone with pleasure! I'm much too busy to pay you any attention, I can assure you. Everything falls on me as usual. Instructions come from Headquarters for immediate attention—officers to be notified—staff for this place appointed—new members enrolled—good heavens, there goes that telephone again——"

She bustled off to her huge desk, where the telephone was imperiously trilling in a clutter of overflowing wire baskets. Thumping herself into her swivel chair she snatched up a pencil and pulled a jotting pad within reach.

"Yes, yes? Ringsey Headquarters. County Secretary speaking.... Yes, of course...quite so...I entirely agree..."

Mary huddled into her corner between a pile of crates and cartons of stationery, bit the end of her pencil and felt both mulish and miserable as she returned to the accounts. She hadn't been sleeping well, lately, an extraordinary thing for her. But ever since Hitler's speech at Nuremberg she had been overwhelmingly aware of the waiting world about her, in the same strange way that she had first been aware of it, on the evening that King George V died. She didn't like it, she hadn't invited it, but there seemed to be nothing she could do about it. The awareness was just there again, gathering in intensity as the days passed, so that she felt like a clock in acute danger of being overwound. For it wasn't only that she, Mary Gordon, was anxious about the safety of her husband and her son. In some odd way she was equally aware of the suspense of millions of mothers; the confused anxieties, the divided loyalties of millions of middle-aged fathers; the rising, tentative, uncertain excitement of millions of idealistic or ambitious young men and women jostling each other at the beginning of their careers.

How could she add up these abominable figures... lists of County Headquarters' Stores... Michael was in Ireland with a party of Cambridge friends... Ted was at sea.... In the awful mood of extended consciousness that she was coming to dread, Mary found herself visualizing the possibility of never seeing either of them again, knowing that with the pictures of sinking ships and diving aircraft and smoking homes and dreadful battlefields she was sharing the thoughts, not only of the women of England but of the women of half the world. She put her hand to her head. It was too much... too much to bear.... Why couldn't she just think of Michael and Ted, as other women did, worrying at least in single-heartedness and privacy? Why did she have to think of the women in France, in Spain, in Russia, in Hitler's Germany, knowing that whatever pretext their leaders might give them, any woman must always in her heart know all conflict to be not only murderous but suicidal.

Those figures..."Due to Wm. Brown, Stationer, Ringsey, for Headquarters Stores"...Michael was in Ireland...was there any chance that he could be persuaded to stop there...those anxious faces against that gaunt building; were they in Germany...in Poland...in Italy...or the U.S.S.R.?..."Quarto paper, headed, twenty-four reams...envelopes, two dozen boxes of two hundred and fifty...half a dozen box files"...Parliament was meeting at that very moment. It was only Wednesday...the suspense seemed to have lasted for years...perhaps there would be something on the news this evening...or a special bulletin...her mother wanted her to check all these wretched items. The paper was all here...envelopes, six thousand cream-laid envelopes...how could they possibly want six thousand envelopes...of course, things would be bound to be short if there was a war. A war...a war...smoke billowing round a newsboy bawling of disaster...Christmas Eve...and a child lying dead among his toys...why had they ever gone to that appalling film about things to come? Years ago now, but she'd never been quite able to get it out of her mind. War...war...war. If the anticipation of it could be like this, then the reality must be quite unbearable. "I shall just go mad and have to be shut up," she thought. "Now for those figures...three and six is nine and four is...thirteen and seven is twenty, and six is..."

Mrs. Prothero put down the receiver. It gave a little chiming ping which made Mary jump. "Tch, tch," said

Mrs. Prothero. "Your nerves, child, must be in a shocking state. Comes of keeping late hours, no doubt. Have you finished yet?"

Counting desperately on her fingers, Mary shook her head.

"Really," scolded Mrs. Prothero, "I don't know where the country's going to be if all the younger women simply lose their heads and can't keep their minds on the simplest duties. There won't be enough of us veterans to leaven the lump if it's quite as doughy as you, Mary. Ted would be furious with you."

"And ten is fifty... and six is fifty-six..."

Mrs. Prothero straightened her tie. She had put on uniform that morning when she got up, for though she really only did three half-days of office work and this wasn't one of them she couldn't be just sitting at home like a civilian on the very day war was likely to be declared. Whatever anybody else did or failed to do, she, Ada Prothero, would be ready at her post. A lucky thing it had been arranged that Mary should come to lunch that day, broken reed though she was. It probably helped Mary too, being with someone who knew how to keep a stiff upper lip when the country's fate was in the scales.

"And nine is twenty-six and five is thirty-one. Put down eleven and carry one...." How well her mother looked. It was impossible to believe she was really seventy. Of course she'd been a good deal younger than her father: she'd enjoyed reminding him of that every now and then. The last few years, Mary realized, as she tapped her pencil against her teeth and watched her mother, must have been hard for her mother to bear. She was one of those Amazonian women who hanker for uniform, and look their best in it. She might have dropped a dozen years as she put on her well-cut tunic. She scarcely looked more than middle-aged. Of course, as far as physical work went, things had been pretty easy for her since the Armistice, with her children settled and other people to do her household jobs, so that she'd nothing to do but give orders to the gardeners, attend her committees and go up to London for conferences, international discussions and occasional shows. No, she certainly hadn't grown old. On the contrary, thought Mary, looking at her mother's massive figure, controlled, almost trim in her navy blue Red Cross uniform with its medal ribbons and epaulettes, her florid features and determined mouth, the wings of grey hair just showing under the uniform hat which she had insisted on wearing all morning, even in her own house; on the contrary, the excitement's doing her good. The chances of war don't worry her. She's tossed it off as a certainty, and it's gone to her head like a pint of champagne.

Hastily Mary brought back her attention to the papers before her, and started muttering again. "Two and nine are eleven and five is sixteen and nine is..." But it was late. Her mother's eyes were upon her.

"Of course, if you can't do a simple thing like that for me, I shall just have to do it myself. As usual. Give these accounts back. At once, please. I, at least, have no time to waste."

"And five is forty. Carry four... carry four... I've just this minute finished," said Mary. "There's the stationery bill, to begin with. It's all right. I checked it. And I've done the bandages and dressings, too."

"Well, I suppose that's something. I shall want all those cartons taken across to the Stores Room. Now. I shall give Mrs. Stokes that to run. She's steady. And she'll keep me in touch. I've got the detachment meeting after tea. I shall tell all the members to consider themselves on a wartime footing. What a mercy the First Aid and Chemical Warfare exams are safely over. We shall turn the Grange into a hospital again, of course. I'm thankful I never let them persuade me that the wards would never be needed any more. I can have them fitted out and in working order before most people have got their curtains down. I shall have to wait for the actual declaration, of course. But it can't be long now. If we're at war by tomorrow..."

Mary watched her with a sort of helpless horror. Could it be possible for a woman who had been through one war already to talk of another and look elated, as happy as a child preparing for a theatrical performance in which she had been promised an important part? Her mother had actually got up from her desk and was peeping at her reflection in the long, gilded wall mirror as she passed it. It was as if she conceived the work of the great international organization of mercy which she served as no more than the prospective setting for her own personal drama. Mary shrank further into her corner as she had the horrible fancy that her mother drew vitality, vampire-like, from the blood bath that threatened the world.

"Really, Mary, if I hadn't just given you a most wholesome and adequate lunch I should have thought that you were either starving or had eaten something that disagreed with you," said Mrs. Prothero. "You're looking as green as a gooseberry. You'd better not start carrying those cartons till you've pulled yourself together. Try the smelling-salts. I keep some in the cupboard behind my desk for beginners at the First Aid classes. They always come over queer when we get to the circulation of the blood. Idiots! But go and get the salts, for goodness sake, and come back and give me a hand with these. Perhaps it's thundery weather. That always made you sick when you were a child—"

"Honestly, Mother, I'm perfectly all right," said Mary desperately.

"All right, you needn't shout. I'm delighted to hear it. You can take this pile, then, and I'll take that. But do let's get started, quick."

She whipped up a pile of cartons and bustled off in the direction of the room marked with the word STORES in scarlet capitals on a postcard. It had once been the library, Mary remembered. Her father had used it as a refuge from his wife's campaigns which frequently swept the house like a whirlwind, retreating into the depths of one of his most comfortable leather armchairs and barricading himself in with half a dozen tomes. Mary could almost fancy that she smelt again the aroma of the special tobacco which he always had blended for him, that he was turning his head towards her to smile and say in a conspiratorial whisper:

"Room for you in this corner, my dear. Out of the draught."

Only, of course, the comfortable chairs weren't there any more. Nor were the big table, the china cabinet, the revolving bookcases that had amused her so much as a child. Even the books from the walls had been thrown into cases and sold. The shelves were stacked with official stationery belonging to this organization or that, with pamphlets, textbooks, examination papers, leaflets and blotting paper. Packing cases covered the bare boards and unshaded electric light bulbs hung from the beautifully molded ceiling with which Mrs. Prothero's activities had been unable to interfere.

Mrs. Prothero, breathless but happy, dumped down her load and looked thoughtfully up at them. "These lights are pretty strong. A lucky thing we've got good thick shutters here for evening work. They're bound to tell us to darken our windows as soon as war's declared." Then she started back again, almost at a run. "Hurry, Mary, hurry," she called over her shoulder. "The detachment will be arriving in an hour or so and there's still so much to be done."

"I was wondering," Mary said, "if we oughtn't to have on the wireless. There might be something—even at the last moment—something that'd stop us having to go to war..."

"Nonsense," said Mrs. Prothero loudly. "No use behaving like an ostrich, my dear. The time for shilly-shallying is over, I devoutly hope. Why, war's probably been declared by now."

"I think I'll go and put on the wireless. There just might be something," Mary insisted. It was probably mere imagination, but the atmosphere felt different about her. Instead of the leaden burden of fear multiplied by millions which had been crushing her she was aware of some other emotion, something that tingled almost electrically, something that felt almost like...hope.

And as she followed her mother through the hall a plump woman in a crumpled cotton frock let her bicycle clash down against one of the stone lions at the bottom of the front door steps. She ran up them calling:

"Mrs. Prothero, Mrs. Prothero...isn't it wonderful... perhaps there won't be a war after all...there's talk of a conference at Munich. Mr. Chamberlain had a message while he was speaking in the House..."

"Oh...thank heaven! Thank heaven!" Mary said. Her eyes had filled with tears but she was laughing as she held both the plump woman's hands, forgetting to weigh the dismemberment of a little country against the peace of the world, remembering merely that there was one of the millions of mothers whose relief she felt sobbing about her, as they dared to think again of the future of their husbands and their sons.

But Mrs. Prothero came out of the Stores Room, moving very slowly, as if she were suddenly tired. Her exuberance had drained from her; she appeared to wilt, to lose her gallant bearing as if a burden had fallen back on her shoulders. She became, as they watched her silently, an old woman, staring blankly past them at the emptiness, the futility, of the coming years.

Mr. Prothero brought his attention back with difficulty from the cosmic splendors of the lecturer's vision. He had been imperiously swept again towards the immensities of eternity, yet these very immensities had been shown him as cradled in the little things of time. All the fragments of medical knowledge he had struggled for, all the scraps the scientists had chipped so laboriously from the overshadowing mysteries, all the less tangible indications of musician or poet, the defiant, illogical convictions of young love, were implicit in the superb conception which had been offered him, as parts of a reality which included every aspect of creation, every intuition of divinity, every hope and dream available to man, no longer clashing and contradicting each other, but blending, each in its place in the cosmos where the links between things visible and invisible, archangel and ant, were forged with an inevitability which chimed like music, fulfilling yet transcending the logical array of data which he had been accustomed to consider the only natural law.

Hugh was waiting for him, looking, as Mr. Prothero muzzily realized, both mischievous and amused.

"I wonder if you'd come and give us a hand in the reception wing, Mr. Prothero," he said.

"Give you a hand in the reception wing?" he said in surprise. "Of course. What's wrong?"

Hugh grinned. "A colleague of yours from over the Border. Never been here before. Can't think what he's doing here now. Thinks he's delirious. Name of Adams, remember?"

"I certainly do," said Mr. Prothero. "The very chap I've been wanting to meet for some little time. He's going to get the shock of his life, I fancy, when he first sees me."

"I rather think he's had it already," Hugh said. "For pity's sake, we don't want him frightened any more."

Mr. Prothero positively winked. "I've hardly dared hope for this moment. But now it's come I'm going to enjoy it. Where's this reception wing of yours? Let's go there—straight away."

Behind one of several doors marked "Consultations" a considerable commotion seemed to be going on. Mr. Prothero looked inquiringly at Hugh, who nodded, then opened the door.

"Tch, tch," said Mr. Prothero. "Dear me." He was aware of amusement, of actual elation, which he recognized as childish, even mischievous, but was quite unable to check.

For Dr. Adams, the physician who had taken such a poor view of Mr. Prothero's prospects, was now evidently taking even a poorer view of his own. He was sitting on a hard chair in the middle of the comfortably furnished consulting room, no longer jovially pompous, but whimpering with panic, his eyes screwed shut and his fingers in his ears.

"All right...all right..." he was roaring incoherently at intervals, "I'm in hell. Why don't you get on with the mumbo jumbo? I'll take it. Bring on the day of judgment and get it over. What're you waiting for?"

On the other side of the big, flat-topped desk a humorous-looking, middle-aged man was watching him with bushy eyebrows raised, apparently waiting for a chance of getting a few words in. He nodded to Mr. Prothero. "Ah, you're a colleague, aren't you? Good. See if you can get him to see some sense. Otherwise I'm afraid we'll have to give him a shot till he quietens down. These confirmed rationalists with a hell-fire background are always the worst at jumping to conclusions. Speak to him, will you? He won't give us a chance."

Mr. Prothero stepped forward and shook Adams by the arm. "Pull yourself together, old chap. You're all right. It's Prothero here."

Abruptly Adams stopped groaning, his eyes opened slightly, his jaw sagged with astonishment. "Prothero! By all that's unholy! So it really is hell—"

"It's nothing of the sort. Just another slight error in diagnosis, old chap," said Mr. Prothero, enjoying himself very much. "You got my chances wrong, too. Done for, I seem to remember, you thought me. Going any time, I believe you said?"

"B-b-but so you were," said the unfortunate Dr. Adams, who had once enjoyed pronouncing death sentences on other people more than he would ever have cared to admit. "And so was I. Couldn't mistake my own symptoms, more's the pity. So of course we must both be in hell..." He shut his eyes tighter than ever, and shuddered from head to foot.

"Stuff and nonsense," said Mr. Prothero vigorously. "This is the best run hospital I've ever come across. I'm taking a post-graduate course here, and you'd better do the same. Remarkable facilities. Consider yourself in luck—"

"In hell—"

"Does it look like hell?" said Mr. Prothero, who had had nearly enough of his joke. "Don't sit there with your eyes shut. Take a look round—"

But Dr. Adams continued to gesticulate wildly, with his eyes tightly shut. "I'm delirious. I'm dying. I'm in hell—"

"We're all pretty busy men here, Adams," said Mr. Prothero, now slightly alarmed by a situation which seemed to be getting out of hand, "so for pity's sake pull yourself together and talk sense."

"I'm damned. I'm damned for ever. I never thought there was any truth in the old tales...but there must be...and of course they've sent me to hell...after all I've said. . . . Go away, Prothero, they've just sent you to torment me . . . isn't it enough to be here?"

Mr. Prothero looked ashamed of himself. Things were going too far. "He really seems to believe it," he said.

"It's not altogether unusual for people to be out of sorts on arrival," said the Reception Officer dryly. "Very common state with intellectual types. Quite unnecessary, of course. This man's religious conceptions are entirely childish, but in point of fact he's capable of really good work. We'd be glad to have him. Dr. Adams, open your eyes—"

"I daren't—all those fiends and flames—"

"You're still obsessed with the nightmare idea you got from that nursemaid," said the Reception Officer kindly. "If you'd only open your eyes you'd see an ordinary consulting room and three ordinary men."

"Go away. I'm in hell. You don't know what I've said in my time. Awful things. About God. Of course I'm in hell—"

"This—this is beyond all joking," said Mr. Prothero. "The man's right out of his mind."

"On the contrary," said the Reception Officer, "he's imprisoned in his own grotesquely infantile conception of the Universe. I'm afraid he's not going to co-operate till he's had a chance of changing his ideas. I'll have to give him a shot. Pity. . . I'd like to have got him on the job at once. We could do with him. Well, there it is."

A nurse appeared as he finished speaking, and deftly contrived to bare an appropriate area on Adams' arm, though at the prick of the needle he set up an inarticulate roar. Then, little by little, his protestations subsided from a roar to a whimper, he lolled sideways, and a couple of attendants appeared with a stretcher trolley, lifted him on it, covered him carefully and wheeled him away.

"Poor chap," said Mr. Prothero. "What on earth went wrong there?"

"Dr. Adams is really a deeply religious man," said the Reception Officer. "And if he had followed the track which was offered him as a small-town practitioner, all his qualities would have worked in together very well. But he was successful and ambitious. He fought his way to Harley Street. He became an eminent consultant. He acquired an enormously hypertrophied intellect while his religious concepts remained as immature as they had been at the age of ten, when a nursemaid frightened him into a neurosis about hell, which arrested all spiritual development. I'd hoped we might be able to short-circuit things by confronting him with a colleague. Well, we hadn't any luck, Mr. Prothero, but thank you all the same."

"I'm afraid I thought too much of settling an old score," said Mr. Prothero ruefully.

"Don't worry. He'll be all right when he's worked things out. We'll be glad to have him with us, too. We're going to need everyone we can get in the Border-line hospitals presently. It's always the same in a war. I must admit the authorities realize the position. They're generous with reinforcements. And a good job, too." He tugged at his thick eyebrows and sighed. "My job's no joke in a war."

But Mr. Prothero was no longer listening. He had turned to Hugh in sudden distress.

"War?" he protested. "War again? I thought we weren't going to have any more?"

"Trouble was, we never finished the last one," Hugh said.

Andrew set his face obstinately against any mention of war. As it came nearer he deliberately refused all speculation, engrossing himself with an increasing passion in the most exacting details of his work on the farm which was his refuge. Michael sensed the change in him most sharply, for, probably without knowing what he was doing and certainly without realizing why, Andrew had set himself to minimize the pain of future partings by withdrawing his attention even from his dearest friend. Turning from human companionship, he found comfort where men have found it ever since history began, in the slow procession of the seasons, the blessed certainty of the rising and the setting of the sun.

When Michael came home from Cambridge, Andrew avoided looking at him; his eyes were anywhere but on Michael's face as they discussed the farm. And Michael, loving his family and his home more deeply than he had ever loved them, was less distressed by Andrew's attitude because he was intuitively aware of the pain which was its cause.

Michael himself had little to say during the summer of 1939, even to Mary. He knew too much to talk optimistically and saw no sense in causing her distress. But he refused all invitations from Cambridge friends for the Easter and long vacations, as if he were determined to spend every waking hour at home. He worked violently with Andrew over all the arduous jobs he could think of, but sometimes he would take a pony and ride for hours over the Forest alone. Sometimes, too, Mary would come on him at odd moments, just standing, watching some ordinary thing as if he could never see enough, for instance, of horses drowsing nose to tail in the orchard, swinging their tails to whisk the flies out of each other's eyes.

One evening she found him leaning over the footbridge that crossed the idle stream that ran, scarfed with white water buttercups, along the foot of the orchard. His pipe was between his teeth but he wasn't smoking it. He seemed to be engrossed in watching the swirl of the water over an outcrop of stone.

"Going to be good for fishing, Mike?"

He shook his head. "Too bright."

"Any good this evening?"

"Maybe."

He wouldn't talk, she knew. But she came and leaned on the rail beside him, and he didn't need to, for she could feel the thoughts that were churning about within him, unspoken, but somehow in the air, rising and blending with the puzzled thoughts of so many millions like him in every threatened country in the world. All those kids—she thought—they felt something momentous coming at them, and they didn't know what to do.

Many she guessed, would not have as much difficulty as Michael. For them the issues were clear. The very danger of war kindled their imagination, so that they turned towards it as the single-hearted had always turned in every generation, because they were young, and adventure loving, and anxious to be brave. And to some, like Andrew, the very thought of it would be horrible, for a variety of reasons, ranging from mere instinctive desire for personal safety to a complex state of conviction which would drive them beyond the shelter of the Services to do all sorts of lonely and conspicuous things.

But Michael, she knew, was not as sure as that. For him the conflict was subtler, because his superb young animal body did not naturally shrink from danger like those of his more sensitive contemporaries, or even men in the forties like Andrew, who had already been once maimed by war. All Michael's fine physical outfit clamored for war's adventures: the recoil came from his spirit alone. His young male strength urged him to fight, for was fighting not part of a man's nature? If there was no war, he would have argued, there had to be hunting and football and boxing and record-breaking to keep people from getting soft. But as far as he himself was concerned, he knew, with a far deeper knowledge than the eager urges of the flesh could ever give, that the love for the land and its creatures which he shared with Andrew belonged to the order of more lasting things. And yet, perhaps...the more dearly loved people or possessions were...the more essential it became to set them free...to lay them down.

"Remember the bit in *Alice Through the Looking Glass,* Mike?" said Mary suddenly. "When she couldn't find her way about the garden?"

"Can't say I do." But the creases on Michael's forehead relaxed a little.

"Well, the more she tried to follow the path to the top of the hill the more she found herself back where she started from. And after a bit she gave up puzzling it out and walked in what seemed completely the opposite direction. And there she was."

Michael took his empty pipe out of his mouth and smiled at her. "How did you know I was trying to work things out?"

"Oh, just the way one does," Mary said. "Supper's ready now. Shall we go in?"

CHAPTER 13

"Harvest should be pretty good this year," Andrew said. "But we're so short of labor I just don't know how we're to get it in."

Michael pondered. "I might be able to get some help, actually," he suggested. "Some of our people would be glad to come. They'd work like blazes, too, even if they looked a bit odd."

"I'd rather hire my own help," Andrew said. "Thanks all the same," he added after a pause.

"All right, all right," said Michael placidly. "If you really get stuck, let me know and I'll see what I can do with the phone."

Getting help didn't prove easy. Men were scarce and the weather was tricky, and when harvest weather eventually came everything had to be done in a rush. So Andrew went reluctantly to Michael.

"Better get those chaps of yours along," he said gloomily. "Board and lodging in the cottage that's empty, usual rates and no fancy airs."

"That'll be all right," Michael said.

He came back from the telephone, after a few false starts, in triumph. "Three strong men and a girl coming on Monday. That do?"

"Can't have the girl."

"Can't help having her, I'm afraid. She's one bloke's sister, and he'd promised to give her a holiday. Poor kid's been stuck in London for years with a dull job and an invalid mother. Mother's gone to Bournemouth now father's retired and her fortnight's holiday's due. He swears she'll jump at this, though. Seems she's nuts on a country life."

"I'm thinking of my harvest," Andrew said glumly.

"Me too. Her brother's one of the best workers I can get you. But he won't come alone. Cheer up, Andrew. Even if she just helps Mum we can't lose by it—"

"Can't we? She'll be the hell of a distraction."

"She's said to be as quiet as a mouse."

"Oh, all right, all right. We'll have her. Don't blame me for what goes wrong."

So Michael's hired help came to the Cherry Orchard, three young men who were to be put up at an empty farm cottage, looked after by the carter's wife and fed at the house. Mary said the girl was different. She would have the second spare room.

"I hope you aren't going to make a fuss of her," grumbled Andrew. "She's come here to work, and work hard."

"If I have any say in my own house," said Mary, "she's going to help me. Mrs. Burns's Bertha's off to camp with the A.T.S. Ridiculous, her mother thinks; the girl's over thirty and says she's twenty-nine. Anyway it leaves Mrs. B. and me on our own, so we'll see this girl's useful all right. What's her name?"

"Something queer," said Michael vaguely. "He did tell me. Wait a bit. Valerie... Hilary... Verity. That's it. Verity's the name."

"Good Lord," said Andrew. "Girl from London called Verity. Won't know which end of a cow does what, and dead certain to slice off a finger when she comes within ten yards of the reaper-and-binder. Charming!"

"If I know anything about Mum, the poor girl's going to be chained to the sink during the hours of daylight," said Michael. "You'll scarcely set eyes on her."

And at first he proved to be right. The three young men from Cambridge, apart from a tendency to sit on after their meals and argue interminably about academic issues, turned out to be a great success. They enjoyed themselves enormously, drank gallons of cider and toiled till the last rays of the sun sent the shadows of the corn sheaves far across the shorn fields. Sometimes they sang, surprising the graver country people with Elizabethan folk songs that had not been heard on these fields for centuries, as the troubles of Europe receded before the needs of the Cherry Orchard harvest. There was no time to go for the papers and the wireless was never turned on. Verity meekly washed dishes and made beds and ran errands and packed lunches and teas for the harvesters and kept in the background with Mary, who grew to love her, wishing only that she could have had a daughter, a serene and golden daughter, just like Verity.

She had been nearly a week at the Cherry Orchard before they discovered her way with animals. Michael had never really noticed her till the day he came up from the field to do the milking at tea time and met Verity who had been picking late raspberries and was on her way to the dairy in search of cream. They looked at each other thoughtfully, but without any disturbance. For the first time they were acutely aware of each other, but aware also that there was no need for either anxiety or pursuit.

It was apparently a commonplace enough encounter. Michael drew the back of his hand across his sweat-blinded eyes, then blinked at her. "Not much fun," he said, "trying to be in two places at once in this heat."

"Couldn't I be in one of them for you?" Verity asked.

"Not unless you can milk."

"I could learn."

"Come and try," Michael said. He grinned to himself as he thought of Andrew's probable reaction. "Ever done any milking before?" he asked, when he had shown her how to set about it and stood back in the dim, sweet-smelling milking shed to encourage her after the expected kicks and blunders. But Verity did not blunder, the cow stood there peacefully, and the milk pinged and purred in two rhythmic streams against the bottom of the pail.

"No, never," said Verity dreamily. Her forehead was resting against the cow's warm flank, her hands worked instinctively, the level of the milk rose steadily in the pail.

"Well, I'll be darned," Michael said. "Well, I'll be darned. Sure you haven't been pulling a fast one on me and worked on a farm for years?"

"I've always wanted to," Verity said.

"You try getting up at five o'clock in the winter—"

"You try strap-hanging in the Tube morning and evening for an hour each way—"

"Rounding up the stock in a downpour with the gateways a foot deep in mire—"

"Groping your way home in a pea-soup fog—"

"The float breaking down on the way to market and your hands so numb you can scarcely change a tire—"

"All jobs are the same that way," Verity said. "You know you've got to take the best with the worst of them, and if you enjoy the work, well, it's always worth while."

"True enough," said Michael gravely.

"You feel like that about farming, don't you?" she asked him.

Michael nodded, chewing a straw. "Best job in the world if you like things this way," he said slowly.

"I bet it is," she said.

"Looks as if I can leave you to get on with it while I take the pails to the dairy now."

"Of course you can," Verity said.

She was cool and completely confident. She did all the milking, stretching cramped fingers between whiles and straightening up occasionally to ease her back. Next time she managed the cows as well, knowing how to round them up and chain them in their places without being shown, placing her stool correctly and settling her pail in a sure sort of way that made Michael feel oddly elated. In a day or two she had found her way into the dairy and been shown how to grade eggs, set cream and make butter by Mrs. Burns, who had never really fancied the work and was getting slower round the house with the years.

And so Michael, who knew efficiency when he saw it, went happily back to the fields, feeling that this, in some odd way, was what had been intended, that even her refusal to try and attract his attention was comforting and right. For, deep in his bones, beyond all superficial feelings, he knew that the relationship between them went far beyond the limitations of a harvest-camp at the Cherry Orchard; that its very lack of stress was a measure of its essential completion, though where, and in what other circumstances, he could not tell.

Mary had a letter from Ted one morning towards the end of August. It was mysterious and rather sinister, full of a certain hush-hush new job on shore. That was the only trouble, he wrote: after all these years at sea it seemed a poor thing to be fobbed off with, but at least it meant a step up, a good deal of responsibility and the chance of seeing them all now and then.

He'd just had her cheery letter about the harvest, and was glad (though reproachful, Mary fancied) that they were all having such a good time. She sounded a bit out of touch with things, of course. Hadn't they been listening to the wireless lately, he wondered? Or reading the papers at all? Seemed odd to get nothing but pages about the harvest party they were having with Michael's queer Cambridge friends. Had they not heard of a place called Danzig? Didn't look as if Michael was going to get that last year at Cambridge, did it? He had the grace not to add that was just what he always said.

Mary pushed the letter hastily into the pocket of her overall and started, feeling thoroughly upset, to clear the breakfast things. Of course, she told herself, Ted simply loved making mysteries. There was nothing new about that. He always had. That hush-hush business was something that seemed to grow on men, she'd noticed, not something they ever outgrew. Ted was getting just a bit heavy and pompous, bless him. He was nearly fifty, too.

And he never even read thrillers or went to crook films or did anything to work the love of mystery out of the system. So he was quite obviously bound to get the last ounce of drama out of life itself. Hadn't they been all living on the edge of a precipice for years? Why should the baseless fabric of world peace sag over the edge just this week? She wouldn't believe him. She wouldn't. She knew far too well what a heavy-handed old sensation monger her Ted was.

So she kept telling herself, clashing the breakfast dishes together on the tray and whisking them out to the scullery, an inconvenient slit of a place in which Mrs. Burns was already monumentally placed between her and the sink, peeling potatoes as if she had a grudge against each one. Mrs. Burns had a husband in the Merchant Navy, Mary remembered, and a boy a year or two older than Michael was. She bit her lip as she stood there in the background, shaking helplessly as she held up the heavy tray, and wondered why she wanted so much to dash it down on the stone floor instead of casually asking good-natured Mrs. Burns to move. She was just being childish, Mary scolded herself, aware of a silly scream rising inside her... irresistibly, like a wave about to break....

But Verity had slipped in behind her. She took first one pile of dishes and then another, said, "Excuse me just a minute, Mrs. B.," and stacked them all beside the sink. Then she took away the tray too, and put it against the wall, tucking her arm under Mary's as she guided her out of the dark scullery and through the house, into the quiet of the long room. The sunshine was streaming in at every open window on to the pleasant, faded chintzes, and the blended fragrance of late roses and lavender came with it as it had come all summer long. Mary wandered to one of the window seats and Verity brought her a cigarette. It shook between her lips as she hunted for her lighter, and Verity struck a match, holding it ready for her, its tiny flame almost invisible, swaying between her cupped hands.

"This is the first I've had for days," Mary said. "I don't really smoke much."

"I know. But sometimes it helps," said Verity.

"I can't think what happened," Mary said. "I'm not usually that sort of a fool. But—I had a letter from my husband—"

She broke off and looked up at Verity, surprised by her protectiveness, her sudden, unexpected strength. Just a kid, she looked, with that slicked short hair, the faded yellow shirt that echoed it and the brown dungarees which were the very color of her eyes. With anybody else she'd have said it was a studied color scheme. But she'd lent the girl the dungarees herself. They were an old pair of Michael's, dating from his second year at school. Perhaps it was the dungarees that made her keep thinking of Mike when she saw Verity. What else could it be? Michael had never looked at the girl twice.

"It wasn't bad news?" asked Verity.

"Well, no. He's all right. But he seemed so sure—so horribly sure—he's expected it for years—"

"The war? Everybody's expecting it any minute, of course. But it may be nothing again. Would he know?"

"He might, I'm afraid."

"You know too, really, don't you?" Verity said.

Mary looked at her, eyes wide, aware of a multitude of impressions which seemed to rush at her from all sides, borne on a tide of uncertainty, whipped to breaking point by panic fear. Desperately she fought them, rejected them, flung them aside, only to be attacked by others which came at her in wave after sullen wave of multitudinous images. Eyes... millions of eyes... eyes poring over precious things suddenly threatened... hands, caressing them, caressing the sleek surface of walnut or rosewood or carved oak, lingering on brocade, plucking at jewels that glowed or sparkled from their nest of velvet... greedy eyes peering into stacked food-cupboards, counting ranked bottles in dusty racks... chalk-white, crimson-nailed hands flicking exquisite clothes from satin hangers... sloe-black eyes snapping... pudgy hands counting notes... work-worn hands dusting grotesque, beloved vases on a suburban mantelpiece... eager hands pushing checks across a bank counter... terror-struck eyes peering through a ticket office window... eyes full of tears watching sleeping children... hands interlaced beside a railway barrier... hands waving, waving, from a slowly moving, inexorable train.

With a little sob Mary covered her own eyes with her hands, swamped by the tide of compassion that swept over her, not only for the obvious losses of people whose fears were her own, but for all the others, the rich, the frightened, the old, the greedy, the people afraid of new conditions, of being alone, of losing their great possessions, faced with the necessity of letting them go or having them snatched from them. Wasn't that the choice that faced everybody? "It's just the same... the same for all of us..." she whispered. She looked up, astonished by the peace that had come upon her. It was as if that admission had dispersed the alien terrors, as her acceptance of it had quenched her own pain.

"Yes, I think I've known quite a long time," she said at last.

"I've known too," said Verity. "At least, I've known something. I wasn't sure what. May I have a cigarette?"

"Of course."

Verity sat down at the other end of the window seat. "It's funny how one knows things. Just sometimes, I mean, like you. I can't think how it happens. I never dream much, do you?"

"Sometimes. But I don't often remember."

"Perhaps that's it," Verity said. "Sometimes in the mornings I feel as if—as if heaven itself were only just on the far side of the door. But before I'm out of bed, it's gone again. All except—you'll think me silly—"

Mary shook her head.

"Well, you remember that old song about a rainbow round someone's shoulder? I heard it revived the other day. It seemed so familiar. Because that's all I ever remember of my dreams. Just something like a rainbow—a promise—that I sometimes get a glimpse of out of the corner of my eyes."

"And I thought you were such a businesslike, practical person." Mary was so surprised that she sounded almost reproachful.

"Oh, but I am," said Verity. "I'm always practical. That's why I've been meaning to ask something. If this happens—if there's a war, Mrs. Gordon—will you let me stay and work here, on the farm?"

"If there's a war, we're certainly going to need someone," Mary said in a flat voice. "Michael's volunteering for the Fleet Air Arm—"

"Yes, I know. My brother told me. He met Michael at the Flying Club, you know. It wasn't because of Michael I wanted to be here," she said frankly. "It's because I think perhaps I'm meant to be here while he's away. I think I might be useful—"

"Useful? Of course."

"But really useful," Verity said gravely. "I could learn to do so much more. I should have to do war work, and I'd love to be here. People might as well do what makes them happy, don't you think? Even in a war?"

"I'm quite sure they should," said Mary, trying not to smile at Verity's troubled face. "The more people who are happy the better, always."

"Even—"

"Especially if there's a war."

"Then you'll have me?"

"I shall love to have you," said Mary, wondering as she spoke why she felt as if her heart had grown lighter inside her. For of course, as they kept telling you in those awful First Aid lectures that her mother was always making her go to, the heart was just a hollow muscular organ situated rather to the left of the chest. So obviously you couldn't feel either joy or pain with it. In spite of what people said. But whatever it was she felt with, she felt better for the thought of Verity being there; Verity, who reminded her so absurdly of Michael... though she never looked Michael's way.

"Of course it's Andrew who runs the farm, so I'll have to tell him," said Mary. "I know it's the animals you really want to work with, isn't it?"

Verity nodded. "Andrew doesn't know what to make of me yet, I'm afraid. He has the gloomiest forebodings!"

"I'll settle Andrew for you," Mary said. "You needn't worry, my dear. He just doesn't notice women. It isn't that he means to be rude."

"I don't care if he looks straight through me always," said Verity. "So long as he lets me work here."

Mr. Prothero stood in a quiet corner of the general recording room, watching the purposeful activity of the men and women who went incessantly to and fro. They moved without haste, but swiftly, coming together into groups to study carefully each swirl on the thunder-dark walls. Everyone, he realized, knew his or her individual job exactly, yet was ready to submerge that individuality without question to the rhythm of a perfectly harmonized whole.

Dark though the place was, it throbbed with confidence. Mr. Prothero felt reassurance come to him as an almost visible glow. He was waiting for James, who was somewhere among the shadows, bustling a little, because he liked feeling important, and Giles, who was working doggedly with Hugh. As he stood there Mr. Prothero became aware of a number of unfamiliar faces, which, once seen, could not be forgotten. The strangers moved unobtrusively among the students and instructors, but there was something different about them, something he found hard to define. It was with a sense of shock that he realized that though there was no light in the place except an occasional smoulder from the wall-maps, he could see their serenely beautiful faces quite clearly, as clearly as if they had been lit from within.

"Who... who are these people?" he asked Hugh, who had just paused beside him.

"Which people?" said Hugh absently. His attention was still on his notes. "Oh, the shining ones. They're reinforcements from headquarters, thank goodness. All Border-line staffs are being enormously strengthened, you know."

"D'you think," said Mr. Prothero rather tentatively, "that there's going to be something I can do?"

"You bet there is," Hugh said. "Where's James? With your experience I expect they'll be glad of you at one of the casualty receiving stations. But James is sure to know. I expect he's gone on already. We'll probably find him in the Central Hall. Come on; I expect you'd like a look round."

"I certainly should," said Mr. Prothero. "I always thought this place was efficient but now there's such a drive on that it makes me feel quite dazed."

Hugh grinned. "Well, it's a crisis, isn't it? And on this side of the Border we've got to keep quite a few jumps ahead."

"That's what it looks like," Mr. Prothero agreed.

As they went from corridor to corridor he was struck by the immense, benevolent efficiency which was evident everywhere; in all the wards, limpid with color, empty and waiting; in all the various departments and their specialist staffs; in the nurses, the doctors, the orderlies; it seemed to vibrate in the very air. The psycho-therapeutic department's galleries had been cleared of bridge tables, magazines and armchairs, and were now equipped as casualty receiving stations.

"Are these for service or civilian casualties?" asked Mr. Prothero.

"We don't have any distinctions here," Hugh explained. "Everything's just mobilized for everybody, you see. You'll get a better idea of the scope of things, though, if we go up to one of the galleries and look down on the Central Hall."

So Mr. Prothero leaned on the balustrade that curved round an arc of the rose-colored shaft under the iridescent, soap-bubble dome and looked silently down on the great nucleus of the hospital's life. Below him the streams of men and women converged, swirled round part of the circumference and set off in new directions. Again, as on his first arrival, he found many of the men and women teasingly familiar, but they were out of sight before he could be sure. Here and there, too, among the purposeful crowds were more strangely shining faces, and Mr. Prothero's eyes followed them eagerly, reluctant to see them go.

As he stood there, he felt the resolution of the whole community rise towards him. They were so calm, so sure. How could they be so sure?

"I can't tell you that," Hugh said, as if he had spoken aloud. "I can't even give you my own certainty. I wish I could. I can only say that we are quite, quite sure of the outcome, even though we're still as much part of the struggle of the world over here as we ever were on the far side of the Border. Our work's different, perhaps, but we're the same. As things go wrong there we're mobilized here to help swing the balance true. You see, really and truly, there's no dividing line between one stage of life and another. There's no frontier except the understanding, no limitations except humanity's faith and hope and—"

Mr. Prothero's attention slid away, as it had always done when he felt people were trying to tell him something he would rather not know. "That's all very well," he said, "but another war means another few million casualties. You can't persuade people to the contrary by any amount of talk about faith and hope."

"I'm not trying to," Hugh said. He looked ruefully at Mr. Prothero. "Only to suggest that death may not matter quite as much as you think. But——" He broke off abruptly. It was expressly laid down in the Charter that only in the greatest emergency might recent arrivals be informed point blank of their new status. It was essential that, if possible, they should be left to realize it for themselves. Understanding might come in a flash, or be obstinately resisted for half a century. Queer how it varied! Young people nearly always tumbled to it at once. Artists, musicians, poets, people with a sense of wonder, guessed pretty soon. The intellectuals were the real problem. He'd known eminent professors and divines be outraged at the unexpected discovery. The scientists and medical men were quite incalculable. Sometimes they took it in their stride, and sometimes they were the worst of all.

"You see," he tried, "life's a tremendous business; we're all part of the same body of creation, whichever side of the Border we're on...."

But Mr. Prothero was not listening.

"I should like to go and see Mary," he said suddenly.

"Why would ye not slip across then, Mr. Prothero?" said James, who had joined them, with the others, unobserved. "It won't be so easy once the trouble starts, but I'd see ye over the Border and she'll be thankful for a sight of ye. Mebbe she'll be scared with things looking so bad."

"The worst time's when they seem to be going well," said Hugh, rather glumly.

"Aye, folk get lulled like, easy to take unawares. Fewer flies get drowned in hot water, Mr. Prothero. They're more likely to be smothered in cream."

"Yes, and I bet the cream's worth it," said Laura. "I used to make a perfect pig of myself over cream."

Mr. Prothero sighed. He had suddenly found himself remembering summer teas at the Cherry Orchard with a pang of longing not only for the sight of his daughter, but for the bland sweetness, just roughened with sugar, of raspberries and cream. . . .

The sinking feeling only lasted for what seemed a few seconds, and when things steadied about him again he was standing in the cool, flagged dairy at the Cherry Orchard, watching Mary skim a great pan of cream. She looked up and smiled.

"Hullo, darling. Come to tea?"

"Yes, I—I believe I have," said Mr. Prothero, in a tone of surprise.

"I'm afraid there's only me," Mary apologized. "Michael's gone off in a hurry to see his father, and Andrew's at market, I think, and it's Verity's free afternoon. Or I wouldn't be doing this. She's marvellous in the dairy."

"It's you I came to see," said Mr. Prothero.

"Then we'll have the last raspberries together. I really picked them for Michael, but he couldn't stay. We got in the last load of barley yesterday, and Michael got hold of a paper today. That was that. Ever since he's thought of nothing but war. Oh dear, I'm so terribly glad to see you, Daddy," Mary said. Her lip quivered a little, and she let her spoon drip a drop of cream on the flagged floor. A little striped cat, which had come in with Mr. Prothero, ran up and licked it passionately. Mary smiled at it as she said: "I can manage, somehow, when we're all together, but I start panicking when I'm alone. It seems like the beginning of something that I mayn't be able to cope with...just the beginning and the end so far away."

Mr. Prothero put his hand on her shoulder. "I know, my dear. I was worried about you. I felt I had to come. Is there any way I can help?"

"Of course you can. Bless you for thinking of it," said Mary. "Let's sit in the long room, shall we? Not outside. It really does look like thunder, and if we carry things into the orchard we'll just have to come rushing in."

It was very peaceful in the long room. Just as usual, thought Mr. Prothero, as he sat down on the couch and waited for Mary to come back from the kitchen. There were bowls of late roses on the desk and table, and trays of lavender and rose petals for pot-pourri were drying on the window seats.

"Not a very good place for them, I'm afraid," Mary said from the doorway. "The cats will jump on them. Verity's going to bring me in another table tomorrow. I won't give up this little one. It's so handy for tea."

Mr. Prothero looked contentedly at his daughter. Mary must be over forty. She had put on weight and Michael pretended to like the touches of grey in her dark hair. But Mr. Prothero still saw the girl he'd given away to Ted Gordon, in the church of St. Michael and All Angels, in October, 1916. Smiling at her as she sat down beside him, he thought how young she looked, how forlorn. He wanted so much to comfort her, but he'd never been an eloquent man: he didn't know what to say.

"It's wonderful to see you," she said. "It seems so long since you've been here. I don't suppose it really is, though. Time's so queer. The clocks say it all goes at the same speed, whatever happens, but it must be nonsense. When I'm talking to you the hands just whirl straight round the clockface, and when I'm waiting for someone they never seem to move at all."

"I'm thankful you've got the Cherry Orchard," said Mr. Prothero. "Funny, you've never wanted anything better, have you?"

"Absolutely never," said Mary. "I don't ever want to be anywhere else. I think I'd be content just to go on doing the usual things here in my sleep or when I died. I belong here. It would have to be something very urgent ever to get me anywhere else."

"A fortunate thing that it's freehold," said Mr. Prothero prosaically.

Mary nodded. "I know, but it isn't just that. It's the sort of place you can be really alive in. We're just like stray cats in London, Andrew and I. Ted's different—he's always been a wanderer, and of course Michael's got to be free. So now, if they take it from us...." She looked round the room, suddenly restless, her fingers drumming uneasily on the couch beside her as they did when she was adding up accounts. Mr. Prothero covered one of her hands with his own, searching for some words of consolation. Then, as he hesitated, he was aware of an unexpected compulsion, and yielding to it he began to speak.

"It's going... to be all right, my dear. It really is. I don't know why I should feel like that. I've been told, but I don't quite remember. I...I know that we aren't left alone. They talked about miracles in the last war. People scoffed, perhaps. But there were...there really were angels at Mons. There always are...they're sent as reinforcements and when we can receive them into our lives...then strange things... very strange things happen. I wish..." said Mr. Prothero, "that I could describe something of what I've seen. But I can't. It's too big." He paused for breath, amazed by the stream of words which seemed to be thrust into his consciousness by an actual outside agency, so that it was less effort to say them than to try and dam them back.

"I just want you to remember, when things seem to be drowning in darkness for you, that there are, there really are great forces working for us, Mary, forces of light that no darkness can comprehend. I...I believe that... that..."

He broke off, as if the unknown compulsion which had driven him to speak so vehemently had now been removed, leaving him at a loss.

Mary turned to him, vivid with hope. "Yes, I know. I believe it too. I'll remember..."

Then her face changed, as if she were listening to some sound he could not hear. Her attention seemed to slip from him. She rose and began to go towards the door, her eyes vague, her hands outstretched as if she were walking in her sleep. Only a whisper reached him as her lips moved: "that telephone...that beastly telephone..."

Suddenly Mr. Prothero became aware that James was standing where Mary had been, with Laura beside him.

"She'll be all right," Laura said gently. "She won't forget now."

"Aye, but ye'll have to be getting back, Mr. Prothero," said James Grant briskly. "Ye're wanted in the casualty receiving station right away."

CHAPTER 14

The telephone was ringing, ringing, ringing...

Mary stumbled downstairs, tugging on a dressing gown, still half asleep, into the dim hall where yesterday's oddments lay about, oddly repellent, grotesquely out of date. There was the newspaper with the shrill headlines; Michael had tossed it down before he left for Portsmouth. An empty glass, rimmed with a lacy crust from last night's beer, stood on the table beside the telephone, and the stale stuffiness of tobacco smoke hung on the air. The polished wood struck coldly at Mary's feet—she might be forty-five, but she had never been able to make herself remember slippers in any crisis—she skidded on a rug and reached the telephone to hear the scared voice of a young maidservant at the Grange asking her to come at once, for Mrs. Prothero had been taken queer. She had left her room in the early morning, it seemed, and started to go downstairs. And then, clutching at a table on the landing to save herself, she must have fallen heavily. The sound of the crashing table had roused the servants on the floor above.

"Ring Dr. Ward at once," Mary said.

"Yes, madam," the girl said. "Oh, but she does look queer. Her face is ever so red, and she can't move or speak to us...."

"I'll come straight round," Mary said. She replaced the receiver, picked up the skirts of her dressing gown and raced upstairs. She must rouse Andrew, and make him start up the car, tell Verity to keep things going, dress and get Andrew to take her to the Grange. It was a stroke, of course. A supremely awful thing for her autocratic mother to endure. It would be difficult to think of anyone who would resent enforced inactivity more. And now, of all times. She remembered her mother's overwhelming disappointment over the resolution of last year's crisis at Munich. What would it mean for her to be struck down now?

But Mrs. Prothero, staring round her ornate, heavily-furnished bedroom with eyes which seemed to be the only living thing about her, was not yet aware, as the wireless gave the news of the Germans' dawn advance into Poland, of the full irony of her position. She thought vaguely that she must be still having a nightmare. Her limbs were leaden; she could scarcely move even a finger. But she knew those sensations. Such absurdities were quite usual in dreams. One side of her face was as stiff as if she had been having a local anaesthetic from the dentist. It would pass, thought Mrs. Prothero. And then, more urgently: it must pass. She had so much, so very much, to do. It was so difficult to concentrate. She kept drifting away from her bedroom at the Grange, from the morning of the first of September, 1939. The people who came and moved her about, who seemed like Dr. Ward, Mary and Andrew, they were just shadows, she could see right through them. They must be parts of the nightmare, too.

She blinked. That was better. She could see more clearly now. Someone was speaking to her, saying: "I'd like you to have a word with the director. Please sit down here."

She knew the voice. It belonged to that long-legged, grave young man who was expected to make such a name for himself. She remembered the fine hands, the impulsive movements, that dark line of moustache above an expressive mouth.... Of course, it was the young surgeon, Thomas Prothero. But surely... surely she knew him better than that... surely he'd asked her to marry him. Oh dear, had she accepted him? Her head was in such a muddle. If he asked her again she'd refuse. She'd had enough of it. It hadn't been any fun, being married to a man whose work came first, last and all the time. She'd been just nowhere. He never thought of anything but his patients and their horrid diseases. And when she forbade him to mention them or think of them once he'd got home, he began to come home less and less.

"Couldn't you have let him talk, shared his interests a little?" That was somebody else speaking, not Thomas. It was a small, brown man with very bright eyes. He wore a beard. And she wasn't in her bedroom after all. She was sitting in what seemed rather like a pleasant consulting room, looking at this stranger across the top of a big flat-topped desk, while Thomas prowled uneasily up and down. For Mr. Prothero had just been summoned from his work in the casualty receiving station, and was feeling restless and distressed.

"He had plenty of time for his interests. I wanted him to share mine," she said. "I wanted him to entertain with me. I wanted him to forget all these miserable people."

"I couldn't," said Thomas Prothero. "I kept hearing their voices in my sleep. They needed so much more help. I couldn't work hard enough...."

"Ridiculous," said Mrs. Prothero sharply. "Surgery's a profession just like any other. What's the use of letting your patients get on your nerves? You had yourself to consider, your wife, your position, your family. I didn't marry a philanthropic institution. I married a man who was gifted enough to be successful, who would support me in the style to which I'd been accustomed..."

"I'd hoped we could work together."

"A woman's contribution is to run her home, to entertain for her husband's advancement, to bring up his children. Isn't that enough?"

"Do you really still think it is?" asked the director.

"What more can any reasonable man want?"

"An exchange, perhaps," said the director. "Supposing your husband were to tell you that social success meant nothing to him. Supposing he were to ask you to start out again. Would you not care to look for understanding, mutual enthusiasms? Could you accept the humble surroundings of a country doctor's practice, I wonder?"

"Certainly not. It would be a wicked waste. Thomas is far too gifted to be buried alive in some wretched damp countryside," said Mrs. Prothero. "Why he might have had a knighthood, even a peerage, if he'd played his cards properly."

"Do these things—really seem of so much greater value to you?"

Mrs. Prothero shot an uneasy glance at the director. How much did he know? Did he guess at the reason for the increasing pace of her social activities, the number of her committees, her patriotic and charitable enterprises? Did he know that all the rest of her life had been one unceasing struggle against the knowledge that she might have been mistaken?

"You are very tired," said the director. "You have been driving yourself too hard. We can offer you the rest you need if you care to come here for treatment."

"Treatment?" said Mrs. Prothero angrily. "There's nothing wrong with me."

"I'm afraid there is," said the director gravely. "The report we have received after your preliminary examination is that the adhesions of an egotistic purpose have so bound down your will that a major operation will be required to liberate it. It has every chance of success, if it is undertaken immediately, but of course it will not be attempted without your consent."

"An operation? What nonsense," said Mrs. Prothero. "I am an extremely busy woman. And since another world war seems liable to break out at any moment, I cannot possibly spare the time for going into a hospital and having unnecessary things done. I am——" she tried to keep the fear out of her voice—"quite indispensable."

"I'm afraid," said the director dryly, "that nobody is. You may refuse the operation we suggest, but you won't be able to avoid the consequences of its necessity. The lesions I speak of are bound to have repercussions on the physical body. They will, in fact, reduce you to complete inactivity. I strongly advise you to come over to us. Don't you agree, Mr. Prothero?"

Mr. Prothero stopped prowling about the room, and ran a hand through his thick, untidy hair as he turned to face his wife. What a child Ada looked, he thought. Just as he had first seen her, pretty as a moss rose and slim as a willow, clapping her hands at life as she saw it from the window of her parents' London drawing room, protected by an expanse of plate glass and lace curtain from all its realities; its stench and its courage and its pain.

"I—certainly—do," he said slowly. "This is a good place, my dear. We—perhaps we could start again together here."

"I don't want to start again," said Mrs. Prothero with a shudder. "Once was enough."

"But, Ada, it would be different. We'd understand more. We could learn together—"

"I don't want to learn. I've got money."

"If you could learn with me, help me—"

"I won't learn." Mrs. Prothero's voice was shrill. "I don't want to know anything about horrors. I won't—"

"Don't scare her, Mr. Prothero," murmured the director.

"But, sir, surely I must make her see—"

"The word 'must' is not used here, Mr. Prothero," said the director quietly. He turned back to Mrs. Prothero. "We can only repeat the offer of skilled treatment, on the condition that you yourself wish to come. If you prefer to return to the old conditions we will help you to do so. But I warn you that you will find them irksome. Will you not trust yourself to us and come?"

"No...no...no!" she said violently. "I don't want to. I won't come. I want to go back..."

"Very well," said the director. "Don't try to urge her further, Mr. Prothero. She has made her choice. There are no merely conventional relationships on this side of the Border. True lovers run together like quicksilver. All others go their different ways."

"Perhaps you'll be kind enough to call me a taxi," said Mrs. Prothero huffily. "As I think I told you, I'm an exceedingly busy woman, Mr.——er——er...."

The director held out his hand. "We won't keep you any longer, Mrs. Prothero. Tell me, can you move..."

"Can you move your fingers, Mrs. Prothero?" Dr. Ward was asking. He was holding her hand in his and speaking very slowly and distinctly.

Mrs. Prothero wanted to say: "Of course. What d'you take me for?" But she couldn't. She couldn't even tell him about the way one side of her face felt. Angry and alarmed, she could only make burbly, inarticulate noises and feebly move the flaccid fingers of her left hand. Her outraged, horrified eyes threatened and implored him, cried out to be delivered from this incredible humiliation, this intolerable bondage.

"That's all right, Mrs. Prothero, I understand," said Dr. Ward soothingly. He laid her hand gently back on the sheet. "Mary, I wonder if I might just have a word with you and Andrew, before I go? They'll be back in a minute," he assured his motionless patient as he followed Mary on to the landing, from which the rise and fall of their voices reached Mrs. Prothero only in a wordless, maddening reiteration. If only she could hear what they were saying... call them back... insist on knowing what decisions were being taken about her welfare. It was absurd, degrading, unthinkable that she should have to lie here, like this. It was unendurable, an imprisonment. Imprisonment? Hadn't somebody warned her of this? Offered her a chance of freedom? Nonsense! It was freedom on her own terms that she wanted, her own familiar life, important and busy, at the center of things. That or nothing, she told herself defiantly. That or nothing. She meant it. They'd soon see.

But the first thing Mary saw was that it would be impossible to leave her mother, helpless and alone, at the Grange, at the mercy of untrained servants. The servants themselves would, in all probability, not be left there long. And she would need nursing, expert nursing, over an indefinite period. Kind, bustling Dr. Ward was not optimistic, could give her no idea of the probable duration of her mother's illness.

"It is impossible to tell, at this stage, the extent of the damage. This stroke may be followed by others. Or she may partially recover. She may be entirely or partly helpless for years. I'm sorry I can give you no more definite idea—"

"I should think," said Andrew harshly, "that she'd rather be dead."

"That's where you're wrong, my lad," said the doctor more cheerfully. "You've no idea of the will that's focused on continued existence in these cases. Otherwise, well, they wouldn't be here."

So the second World War began for Mary, not as a new adventure which summoned all her courage and resource to deal with strange and stimulating problems, but merely as a series of domestic emergencies which demanded that she should continue to run her household under conditions which became more and more exacting as petrol and food were rationed, servants called up, shop deliveries discontinued, and minor exasperations multiplied.

Even the knowledge that Michael had volunteered to serve as a pilot with the Fleet Air Arm was ousted from first place in her consciousness during the weeks that followed, by the necessity of making immediate and complicated arrangements to have her mother moved by ambulance to the Cherry Orchard in order to exchange the appalling prospect of running two households for the slightly more manageable task of adding a helpless invalid, the necessary nurses and all their equipment to the household which she already ran. Her mother, lying like a log, life only apparent in her desperate eyes, was understood to give her consent to the move, and for the next few weeks it seemed to Mary that she herself never stopped running up and down stairs, or acting as a buffer between ill-assorted members of her domestic staff.

Michael had come back, tense, but elated, from his interview with the Selection Board, but she seemed to have very little time even to discuss future developments with him, or to hear more than a brief outline of question and reply, with thumbnail sketches of the officers who had conducted the interview.

"I'm either soothing nurse, or comforting Mrs. Burns," she said to Verity one evening, "or getting the new maids settled, or ringing the Red Cross people about taking over the Grange, or trying to find something that Mother would like me to read her from the paper, or signing forms, or getting food, or helping to fit people with gas masks or get evacuees into other people's houses. And from the way some of the householders look at me you'd think they suspected me of landing myself with two nurses and an invalid just to get out of having them in mine."

Verity, calm as usual, smiled. "But you aren't getting nearly enough work out of me," she said. "I could perfectly well do the shopping when I take the van in to market."

"My dear, could you really? It'd be wonderful if we could get some sort of system into things," said Mary gratefully, thanking her stars that at least the war, which had brought so many horrors, had also brought Verity. For Verity moved serenely about the place, unruffled by anything, dealing with the cows and the dairy and the poultry and the pigs, driving the van to market and managing

Andrew with a skill so great that it never obtruded itself, a compassionate understanding of his need for refuge which made her part of that refuge herself.

For this Mary was thankful. She had dreaded Andrew's reaction to the declaration of war and for this reason she had involved him as much as possible in all the decisions which their mother's illness made necessary, keeping him with her and consulting him continually, so that he had less time to think about the desolation that war must bring. In a sense the Cherry Orchard had already been left desolate. For since Michael had been told by the president of the Selection Board at the end of his interview that he would be recommended for a pilot's training, only his outward semblance seemed to have returned to the farm, there to wait impatiently for the final summons. It was as if the center of his whole life had shifted, had already reached out so far into the future that he dared not turn back into the past.

So Michael did the jobs which were offered him, but without any of the old zest. It was Verity who pored over catalogues with Andrew, discussed prices, reminded him of letters and telephone calls, and filled in an ever-increasing sheaf of forms. For his mother, Michael's restless presence was so much of a mockery that when he left at the beginning of October to begin his initial training at the Royal Naval Barracks, Mary found it an actual relief not to have him prowling about the place like a body without a spirit, waylaying her occasionally with troubled questions, asking her anxiously whether anything could have happened to his papers, or whether she thought perhaps they didn't want him for the Fleet Air Arm after all.

After he had gone Andrew seemed, superficially at least, almost to forget him as the months went by, and the phoney war of 1939 became war in earnest in 1940. He was working fanatically; and he worried her, too, by his refusal to talk to anybody about Michael, or to say what he really felt about the war.

Dr. Ward, on the other hand, did not take a very serious view of it when she spoke to him about Andrew after one of his visits to Mrs. Prothero.

"I shouldn't worry too much, my dear. He's got a fine, wholesome life, with plenty of open-air activity, and his family about him. It's exactly what he needs. He's better here than anywhere else. After all, his work's of national importance now, and it isn't as if there were any chance of anything or anybody turning up that'd be likely to recall that bit of trouble he had last time. I shouldn't care to say what might happen if he were in London, now that so much bombing's going on there. But down here, well, what could be more normal, more peaceful? He's a jolly lucky chap. Just you let him carry on, Mary, and don't fuss yourself about him. If he wants to work hard, let him. We've all got to work hard now."

"There's something in that," Mary agreed.

"And how's it suiting you?"

"Very well indeed. I've lost pounds already."

"Huh, I've no patience with this craze for being slim. Better fat and healthy. What's the news of Michael? Good?"

"Yes, splendid. He's practically through his training, I gather, and he seems to have had a wonderful time. Everything's wizard, including everything at Greenwich, and he's due to be posted any time, to an aircraft carrier, apparently. He's been flying fighters, you see."

"Taken to it well, hasn't he?" said Dr. Ward. "I'm surprised, I must say. I was prepared for him to be wretched, knowing what he felt about the land."

"Mike's an odd boy," Mary said. "He's always been a bit of a philosopher. He'll fight like mad to keep something he values as long as he sees there's the slightest chance of success. But then he never hangs back from the inevitable. He throws himself into it head first."

"Quite so, quite so," said Dr. Ward.

"Tell me, how's your wife getting on these days?" Mary asked.

"Not too grand, I'm afraid. Can't seem to rouse herself. But Joanna, now——" The doctor's tired face brightened. "It's an odd thing about her. You know the way she's been mooning about ever since young Hugh's accident? Well, when the blitz on London started she began to take notice again. And one day she suddenly snapped out of it all and went off to join the Civil Defence. Just like that. Seems to suit her down to the ground. She's a different creature. Writes regularly. Comes down for her week ends off. Sleeps the clock round."

"I'm terribly glad," Mary said.

"Probably went hoping to get bumped off in the first place," admitted Joanna's father, rather grimly. "But she seems to have got over that idea now. Weight off my mind, I admit."

He looked at his watch and began to bustle. "Well, my dear, mustn't keep you. Got to be getting on myself. We aren't doing so badly, any of us. We're through the worst now, I shouldn't wonder. Won't be long before we get them on the run."

The sound of his voice floated up to the pleasant front bedroom that Mary had surrendered to her mother, and which now bore the unmistakable imprint of the highly trained, extremely competent hospital nurse on every austere inch of it, from the bare boards, exactly opened windows, and precisely disposed trays of bowls and dishes covered with clean cloths, to the faint suggestion of disinfectant which hung, night and day, on the air. In winter a small fire burned in the grate: in summer it was replaced by a fan-shaped decoration of folded paper. Seasonable flowers stood on the central table all the year round. They were carried in first thing in the morning and carried out last thing at night.

Every morning Mary came in and made conversation after breakfast. Sometimes Mrs. Prothero was glad of this, and sometimes she felt she couldn't bear a single word. When this happened she could only shut her eyes and make strange little sounds like an angry animal, in spite of which Mary sometimes stayed on, making desperate comments on the war or the weather, till eventually, feeling wretched and illogically guilty, she would let herself be driven away. But she always came back after lunch with the paper and doggedly read it aloud. Dr. Ward had said it was good for her mother to be kept in touch with things, however much of a mockery it seemed.

So Mary had gone on reading the leading article and some of the news items all through the Battle of Britain and the dark time which followed, when there seemed to be no steadfast light left on the continent of Europe, nothing but little flames of insensate courage which, like the wild flowers of the London ruins, kept cropping up in the most unlikely places and saving the world from the dark.

And Mrs. Prothero lay there, with only her eyes, it seemed, alive. The stream of words flowed round her, teasing her like a cloud of gnats. She did not understand them, quite often. They seemed to have so little meaning now, for once the place she had made for herself at the center of the drama had been taken from her, the drama itself lost both reality and purpose. All her vitality, deprived of its opportunity for dominance, was now involved in the struggle to regain control of her body, which, instead of being her obedient instrument, now encased her as if in lead, more helpless and humiliated than a medieval knight sent sprawling in full armor, to be the laughing-stock of any nimble child.

Jane Oliver

Sometimes, during the long nights when she lay wakeful, she thought she heard people talking to her from the far side of the shadows that lay thick about the room. But of course she must just have been dreaming, and anyway, they'd been talking nonsense. Absurd to tell her that she could get up and walk, there and then, if she wanted to, that she need only abandon the futile struggle to regain control of her body and come to them, over the Border where the edge of the morning began. Very pretty, perhaps, but nonsense. Nonsense. Not a word of truth in it. How could there be? These were just fevered imaginings, suicidal impulses. Whatever happened, she would never yield, she told herself. Never. They'd always told her that she had a strong will. It was still strong. Stronger than ever. She would win.

Desperately she tried again, bringing all her will power to bear on the puffy, carefully tended hand that lay uselessly outside the bedclothes, unable even now to believe that the concentrated violence of her personality could not produce response from finger or toe. Her will, that ungovernable, self-obsessed will which had dictated the entire course of her life, from the first pretty whims of a rich man's spoiled daughter to the grimmer, driving passion of a lonely, ageing woman, now seemed only to recoil on her baffled, shrinking spirit. Tears gathered under her closed lids, tears of self-pity and weakness that spilled from her eyes and coursed down her contorted face till they dropped from her cheek on to the pillow. It was easier, somehow, now that she had let herself cry. Then, disconcerted, she realized that she was no longer alone in the room. Someone had seen her weakness, was even mopping at her wet face. Within her unresponding body Mrs. Prothero shrank away, wretched with shame at the idea of any of her family even suspecting her of tears. But perhaps it was only Nurse. That wouldn't matter. Nurses were employed to humiliate you. She ventured to open her eyes. It was not the nurse. But it wasn't Mary either, fortunately. It was just that land girl they called Verity.

Verity said nothing as she put the handkerchief away. She stood quietly beside the bed, silent and unsmiling. But in some odd way something like comfort seemed to come from her, warm like the first light of morning or the evening welcome of a wood fire. Her brown eyes, warm and dark, seemed bigger with unshed tears as she looked down at Mrs. Prothero, but she made neither sound nor movement, and her bare arms hung loosely by her sides. Mrs. Prothero liked looking at her, though she couldn't imagine why. The girl was not specially pretty. And she was only wearing ordinary brown dungarees with an open-necked blue shirt. Her hair was rather untidy, plastered damply round her forehead by a shower of rain and curling up in peaks from the nape of her neck. But as she looked at Verity it ceased to matter that the girl had found her defeated and crying. Nothing, not even her bitter humiliation, was hurting quite as much as it had once done.

Slowly she became aware that an exquisite sense of relaxation had begun to steal over her. The futile, exhausting struggle for mastery no longer seemed essential, and as she ceased to strain against her imprisonment she had her first glimpse of the possibility of freedom, a freedom that lay, paradoxically, beyond the utter surrender of her broken spirit. It was a sight so strange that she could only bear it for an instant. But the memory of its promise lingered as her eyelids dropped again. She fell asleep.

CHAPTER 15

For Mr. Prothero, the last vestige of coherence seemed to leave the time sequence of his existence as everyone about him swept into action against the world emergency. He had no longer time to wonder at the strangeness of unremembered comings and goings, no longer the self-obsession to worry about his own mental state. He, too, was needed, it seemed, though at first he scarcely understood in what capacity. The need was enough. It mattered less that he did not understand. He was caught up in the rescue squads which surged irresistibly across the Border, to break against the terror of the world's darkness like a wave of light.

Whenever he crossed the Border during the war years Mr. Prothero felt as if he were battling his way through the choking smoke of sinister conflagrations, smoke so dense that he was scarcely aware of the presence of his companions, still less of their whereabouts. Sometimes, as the sullen wreaths blew apart, he caught a glimpse of James's reassuring grin, heard his excited voice above the pandemonium of fiendish sound, the drum roll of his r's and the good Scots idiom of his childhood asserting itself in crisis, his untidy hair standing up on end.

It was hard to say whether it was day or night. Sometimes it might have been one and sometimes the other. Fires made the sky lurid as red-hot metal, darkness came down like an intermittent pall. Mr. Prothero had no idea where he was, only that he came and went between the hospital's blessed tranquillity and the shrieking chaos of something like another world. Now and then he thought he recognized a dome or spire that suggested London, a ponderous building which might have belonged to Berlin, a few battered landmarks which might have indicated Coventry or Hamburg, Brussels, Amsterdam or Stalingrad, Portsmouth, Frankfurt, or Exeter. It didn't seem to matter any more. The maimed, the terrified, the dying, were everywhere, their needs no greater in one country than in another. With James and Laura, Giles and Hugh, and among a host of others whom he scarcely knew, he plunged through acres of desolation in search of the injured who had no other rescuers.

Soon he ceased to question the strangeness of it all, though he thought he must be becoming lightheaded when he caught glimpses of the winged figures of the shining ones moving serenely through darkness and flame. Sometimes he fancied that the man he had supposed to be the gardener was also among them, but the light seared his eyes, so that he could not be sure.

Joanna's ambulance jolted over the cobbles into the yard as she came back from a call. Under the archway where the vehicles were kept a blue light was always burning. She backed the big Ford carefully into its position in the front rank. Her attendant collected case-sheet and first aid kit, they went to the office together to make their report, then to the improvised canteen where other drivers and attendants were already drinking cups of tea.

"Had a good trip?"

Joanna pushed her tin hat to the back of her head, and nodded. "Not so bad."

"Casualties?"

"Three. The rest were sitting-cases. They went in the cars. Any tea going? Thanks."

Mr. Prothero would scarcely have known her. Her hair no longer hung limply about her shoulder, but curled all over her head. Her tired face was carefully made up, and she no longer sagged, but stood sturdily in her heavy boots. "My clutch is slipping again," she said to the man who had offered her a cigarette. "Remind me to report it in the morning."

When she finished her cigarette she stubbed the end out under her heel, clashed her empty cup on to the tray among the others, and went yawning to the corner where the bed she had not yet had a chance to sleep in was made up on a stretcher. The All Clear sounded as she worked her way out of her gum boots. It was four o'clock. She hung her tunic on the back of a chair, rolled between the rough blankets and was instantly asleep.

"Hullo, darling. That clutch of yours is slipping like hell," Hugh said.

Joanna's smile was awed. "I don't give a damn about the clutch, but I never get used to finding you there. Just there, beside me—"

"I've been there quite a while, believe me," said Hugh.

"I thought you were. Did you know I was scared?"

"You were fine."

"I was terrified."

"That doesn't matter. Not if you keep on."

"Of course. What else can I do, now I know you're all right? Hugh—"

"Yes, darling?"

"You'll still be about next time I'm on duty?"

"Sure."

Morning for Mr. Prothero

The girl on the next stretcher propped herself up on one elbow as the deep tones of Big Ben reverberated through the common room. It was morning again. Cracks of sunlight were showing round the edges of the stifling black-out curtains, and the people on the early shift were coming round with cups of tea.

"Talking in your sleep again, Joanna," she said lazily, as she reached for a cigarette. "Who's Hugh?"

Things had eased off in the casualty receiving departments and Mr. Prothero had come out for a look round when he met Hugh on the way from the special recording room. His face was grave.

"It's Andrew," he said.

Mr. Prothero fell into step beside him. "What's wrong?"

"Helen Delamere. Remember?"

"But she's married to somebody or other with a title in the Midlands. Right off the map, I thought."

"She's divorced her commercial baronet under the Herbert Act," Hugh explained. "She's had a wretched life with him, and it hasn't done her any good. She's out after any excitement nowadays. So when she sees Andrew—"

"But isn't she still in the Midlands?"

"She's spending a week end with friends at Ringsey. It looks like sheer chance. It isn't, of course. The other side are trying to break down the bridge—"

"The bridge?"

"The bridge that carried Andrew across the shell-shocked years. His memory's a blank between 1915 and 1920, you see, so Helen Delamere comes into the missing bit. If she tries to make him remember his infatuation for her she'll also be breaking down the bridge. And if she succeeds she may break down his sanity too."

"Good heavens, can't you prevent it?"

Hugh shook his head. "I doubt it. People are free. Of course, there's always Verity...."

"Verity? What can she do?"

"Quite a bit, maybe. If she'd stay on over there and help Andrew for a while it might make all the difference. She's just balanced between night and morning, you see, almost ready to take the next step. The thing is, of course, that people at that stage mustn't see where that step's going to lead them, for if they move in the right direction for the wrong reason it won't bring them here at all."

"Tch, tch," said Mr. Prothero, quite out of his depth.

Hugh grinned. "They've got to take the step into the morning, you see, without hoping to gain anything from it, even believing that it may lead them, for the sake of someone else, straight back into the night."

But Mr. Prothero was no longer interested. "I don't know what you're talking about," he said. "What's going to happen to Andrew now?"

Morning for Mr. Prothero

Andrew stood on the warm cobbles of the Market Square at Ringsey, and all the cheerful tumult of Thursday's market mounted round him as he waited for Verity. He glanced contentedly about him, taking in every detail of the familiar scene. The bellowing, cackling, bleating, barking and shouting was going on as it had done every Thursday for centuries, even in the invasion summer of 1944. He loved every aspect of it; the stalls of garden produce, the ranked cages of fowls; the pens in which protesting cattle, sheep and pigs awaited a change of ownership, prodded and pondered over by the local farmers and small holders in their ancient, weather-worn clothes; the booths which displayed cheap, bright blouses, tawdry scarves, jewelry and handbags for the women, the saddlery and farm utensils, from ploughs to milking stools, laid out on the steps of the Market Cross. Each stall had its cluster of people round it, while a more businesslike group followed the auctioneer, already hoarse and red from bawling, as he went from pen to pen.

Andrew did not notice that a large car, with a W.V.S. sticker on its windscreen, had drawn up on the far side of the street. He had no idea that the woman in it was watching him intently, nor any way of knowing that she had heard his name mentioned at dinner the evening before, and afterwards questioned her week-end hostess as to what Andrew Prothero was doing these days and where he was most likely to be found. She seemed to be still pondering as she watched him from under half-closed lids. Then suddenly she threw the half-smoked cigarette into the gutter and slid out of the car.

She was tall and haggard, beautifully turned out in black and looking about as out of place among the homely country women as a whipped-cream confection among cottage loaves. Andrew saw her come towards him with indifference. Then he looked at his watch. If Verity didn't come soon he'd have to decide on those cows without her. A pity to risk letting them go. But Verity, he knew, had a pretty shrewd eye for a good milker. Perhaps—

"Well, Andrew," said a lazy voice beside him, "this isn't much of a welcome, I must say."

Andrew whipped round, stupefied with astonishment, clutching at his old hat, his face still blank. "I'm most awfully sorry, but I'm afraid—"

"My dear Andrew, what nonsense this is—"

"You've got me mixed up with someone else." There was a note of desperation in Andrew's voice. He was sweating now with embarrassment, and something else... something else he hadn't yet recognized as fear. But the low, husky voice went inexorably on.

"No, I haven't mixed you up with anybody. You're Andrew Prothero, aren't you?"

"Yes—"

"Well, I'm—Helen."

"I still don't—"

"Don't remember Helen Delamere? Oh, come. I don't believe you'd be so dumb. You aren't trying to be awkward, by any chance, are you?"

"No, of course not, honestly. I just don't know—"

Lady Hornsey laid two cold fingers on Andrew's wrist. "Listen. It oughtn't to be so hard to remind you. My name's Hornsey now—"

"Hornsey... Hornsey..." Andrew repeated it wretchedly, racking his brains for a clue.

"But that's all over. I'm still Helen. Does that really tell you nothing? Nothing about the good times we had together in London—this dates us a bit, doesn't it, but never mind—back in the last war? That night we danced at the Savoy and you brought me orchids, orchids with a blue velvet case tucked among the petals. It was a ring, Andrew, a diamond and sapphire ring.... Yes, I thought that would bring it back to you... I thought you couldn't really forget...." Her voice had an edge of cruelty, as if whether she actually knew what she was doing or not, her instinct was to wreck, to tear at the security of someone who had dared to rebuild his life without her, while she was still living in the ruins of her own.

Andrew felt the sunny, safe Market Square shudder about him. Darkness seemed to rush over the sun. Pain stabbed at his head... pain... nausea... terror... terror and icy cold, arctic darkness... darkness in which a man's soul might drown. With a little cry he flung up his hands as if to shield his face.

Jane Oliver

Then, through the tumult, he heard Verity's quiet voice. She was beside him. Her hands had closed on his clenched fists; she pulled them gently down, then held them, held them firm and hard. Her hands were warm, living, real. He drew a deep, gasping breath of relief.

"So sorry to be late, Andrew," Verity was saying. "The beastly lorry broke down and there I was with six pigs and everybody shouting at me. Luckily I had a petrol tin...."

Slowly Andrew felt himself swim up towards the surface. Light glimmered above him. Verity's voice, clear and steady, reached him like a shaft of sunshine.

"I'm afraid I don't know who you are," she was saying to someone else. "But this is a friend of mine. He hasn't been very well, you see. I think if I were you I should go. I'll see he gets home."

Andrew blinked. Slowly things came together again. He was standing in the sunlit Market Square with all the familiar sights and sounds about him. Verity was still holding his hands. On the far side of the street a powerful car was starting up with a burst of acceleration that was like machine-gun fire. Andrew winced. "What happened? I feel all muzzy," he said.

"Expect you've eaten something that disagreed with you," said Verity. "In this weather, it could scarcely be a touch of the sun. Today's the first time we've seen it for weeks. All right now?"

"Fine," said Andrew vaguely. "Glad you came along. I want you to come and look at those heifers."

"Before we look at anything," said Verity with decision, "you're coming right along with me to have a really good lunch. I can't bear being as hungry as this for one minute longer."

"All right, all right," Andrew said, grinning as he led the way to the inn.

Round them at lunch the talk of the progress of the invasion of Europe was mixed up with the prospects of the harvest, with cautious hopes for an early end to hostilities and complaints of the increasing number of forms that a man had to fill in before he could even farm his own land. Andrew did not talk much, but Verity, watching him carefully, felt that this was not from any unusual cause.

"Got a headache?" she asked him as they left the shadowy coffee room.

"A bit."

"We'll get the business done and go home early, shall we? I think it's thundery myself."

"Those heifers..." said Andrew doggedly.

"All right, we'll go and see them straight away."

They were back in the lorry sooner than Verity had dared to hope, bouncing over the uneven wartime roads back to the Cherry Orchard. Andrew was quite ready to let her drive. He felt leaden with fatigue, as he slumped back in the corner of the driving cabin, falling out of one uneasy doze into another, opening his eyes between whiles as if to reassure himself that Verity was really there.

In the general recording room it was no longer dark. The walls blazed and glowed as the vivid tide of color reached out towards the sullen, clotted shadows, like molten lava surging over inimical rocks and kindling everything combustible in its path. But as the brightness swept on, those areas that had previously glowed most staunchly in the darkness seemed to dim and flicker, as if exhausted, the splendor drained out of them, as if it had been choked under its own ash.

"The worst time's still to come," Hugh said as he stood beside Mr. Prothero, watching new lands cascading into illumination, then subsiding into a queasy alternation of light and darkness that threatened their new brightness with reactionary excess. "Looks as if there's going to be the heck of an overswing almost everywhere."

"Well, of course," Giles said philosophically. "Have to allow for reaction, you know."

"Longer queues and shorter rations than ever," Laura said. "Half the world starving and the other half tired of going short."

"People are going to get angry now they aren't scared any more."

"We're going to hear quite a bit about the species called spivs."

"They're all feeling older."

"They're terribly tired."

"And yet—peace, peace at last," said Mr. Prothero. "Surely everybody's going to be thankful for that?"

MORNING FOR MR. PROTHERO

"Ye'd be surprised," said James, smiling crookedly, "how much they'll find to grumble about, just the same."

"And besides, it isn't peace yet, not by a long chalk," Giles said. "More than you think may turn on the way the Far East's war's won."

"The Far East," said Mr. Prothero. "No...I hadn't forgotten that."

For Michael was due to go out East soon, to fly carrier-borne aircraft, Bill said, in the offensive against Japan. Bill was only occasionally in the recording rooms nowadays, since his assignments with the fighting men still kept him fully occupied, but sometimes he would go to a screen and flick on a record of Michael's squadron, explaining that in wartime these groups of young men had achieved such a degree of unity that it was often difficult to assess the life of any one of them apart from the lives of his friends.

Mr. Prothero had taken one long look at the complex of interlacing, vivid colors which had been evolved under the stress of danger and in the constant presence of death. It formed a pattern of such strength and beauty that he realized for the first time what a lovely thing a corporate entity might be.

And then he had moved away, not caring to study the screen in detail, picking the pattern apart as Bill did, indefatigably checking with the others who worked beside him every potential crisis point in each fighting man's destiny. Instead, Mr. Prothero found that as he thought of his grandson he was coming more and more to abandon all attempts to trace the interlacing of the forces that helped or threatened him. He scarcely realized how earnestly, yet how secretly, he had begun to pray.

One day Mary got news that Ted and Michael were both coming on leave at the end of the week, and all other considerations were at once submerged in preparation for them. Ted arrived the day before Michael. He was very much the senior officer now, Mary thought. Odd to think that he was only a few years older than Andrew, who still seemed, in spite of the meshwork of lines at the corners of his eyes and the traces of gray in his fair hair, so much like the young brother she had bossed and been responsible for so many years ago. Michael was lean and brown and quiet, and it was Ted who told Mary that his leave probably meant that he was going to be sent to the Far East.

"Inevitable, of course, sooner or later. We're bound to need all our carrier-borne aircraft for Pacific operations. Mike's had a lot of experience now, you know." Ted sounded proud and pleased.

"Yes, I know," Mary said.

But she was glad to think that the differences between father and son had at least been forgotten. Ted was enjoying himself so much, discoursing on naval strategy for the benefit of the two other men while she and Verity got Nurse's tray or helped Mrs. Burns with the washing-up.

Andrew and Michael, very moderately interested, sat smoking and putting in an occasional word till the twilight blurred Ted's elaborate dispositions on the tablecloth, and Verity looked in to ask if they could all do with a cup of tea.

Michael did not, as a general rule, see more of Verity than of the others. Between the two of them, habitually, an odd peace lay, so that, though they did not say much to each other, the same ideas often came and went between them, and they sometimes secretly smiled, each as aware of the other's thoughts as if they had been exchanged aloud.

But on the morning that Michael was due to go back to duty Verity got up at five to go down to the ten-acre meadow and look for early mushrooms. Michael, unable for once to sleep the clock round, had given it up at first light and gone out to walk about the place and look at things and think. And so it happened that he came upon Verity, dew-darkened dungarees clinging to her ankles, stooping busily about the ten-acre field. He did not go to her, but sat on the stile and waited, an empty pipe between his teeth. Some of the hollow feeling round his heart seemed to leave him just because she was there.

When she had nearly reached the stile she looked up and saw him, waved and came on, pausing to pick a few last mushrooms on the way. As she reached him he put out both his hands. Very deliberately Verity set down her basket and laid her wet palms on his.

"Funny," he said, "I've never even touched you before."

"It—it didn't seem to matter, did it?"

"But it's rather nice—now."

"It's going to be all right, Mike," Verity said.

"I know. But going back this time's different. I'm scared. It was so queer, seeing you just now. Like going back into my dream."

"Or forward," Verity said gravely. "I'll be there too, you know. Whatever happens."

"Yes, I know. But Verity, there's one thing—"

"About Andrew?"

"Yes, I thought you'd know," Michael said. "Be good to him, Verity. He's a grand chap. And this—this is going to hit him. He and I set quite a bit of store by each other—"

"Of course."

"He's had a pretty tough time, I gather. I feel—well—rather as if he couldn't cope with very much more. If he had any tougher bits to work out on his own, somehow, I doubt if he could make it, that's all."

Michael's troubled eyes watched the level beams of sunlight reach down the long meadow towards them like fingers of glory. But he sought in vain for words which would adequately express the love and apprehension that he felt for his friend.

"It's all right, Mike," said Verity simply. "I won't leave him to try and work it out on his own."

"Bless you...my darling," said Michael deliberately, peaceful again as he drew her towards him. He could feel the strength of her warm young body now from breast to knee, but the lips he gently touched with his own were cool as ever. "I've never made love to you before," Michael said. "And now I can't bear to say good-bye."

"You needn't," Verity said earnestly. "Never, Mike. I know that. But I don't know how or why."

"It's all so queer, Verity," said Michael wonderingly. "When I say that you're very, very dear to me, it's true. But it's not all. Not nearly all. I can't say good-bye to you any more than I could say it to myself. Don't let's talk about it. I want things to be absolutely ordinary, this morning, right up to where I have to go."

"I'd like it that way too," said Verity.

CHAPTER 16

Michael's hands were so cold he could scarcely feel the controls. He must have lost quite a bit of blood, he guessed, from the Jap gunner's lucky burst that had smashed his r/t and peppered his shoulders. Couldn't really have done so much damage, though, or his arms would be useless. Not just stiff and numb. He couldn't feel any pain, so perhaps it was only the cold. He'd still got a lot of height. The shifting clouds below him heaved like dirty soapsuds. Every now and then a gap appeared, and he caught a glimpse of wrinkled, inimical sea. What a lot of tripe they talked about the Pacific being always blue. They'd have to rewrite some of those travel folders once the boys got home.

Home... with the war in Europe obviously in its last hours that very week end. What were they doing now, back home? How many people were still thinking of the boys sweating across Burma or trying to shoot the Japs out of the sky? Quite a few, he guessed, after all. Early summer evening in England now, when you'd done all the calculations and remembered double summer time; hawthorn still loading the hedges round the Cherry Orchard, the dogs barking at some imagined nonsense; Mum and Andrew and Verity sitting over supper... Dad probably on duty.

Mechanically he checked over the dials on the dashboard of his single-seater fighter. Everything was okay. He should get back, on the whole, he thought. He'd been given a bearing just before that yellow bastard got him, and the aircraft was fine. If only he wasn't so cold. It was getting dark, too. Must be the hell of a storm coming. Well, if his usual luck held he'd be snug between decks by the time it broke. Couldn't be far now. That buzzing in his ears probably hadn't anything to do with the engine. Might be running out of oxygen. Didn't matter, though. He'd soon be down.

Good to be back on board after a long trip, good to ease up in the Ward Room and hear the boys swopping experiences over the medley of companionable noise. Good to have someone to talk to; you got fanciful after you'd been too long on your own. Thought you heard all sorts of things, now and then, things that you didn't care to tell people about afterwards for fear they'd think you nuts. Voices... it was the loneliness that did it, of course. Made you imagine things....

"All right, old boy. Keep her steady...."

"Hullo, that you again?"

"Okay. It's Bill."

"Good to have you to talk to. I'm...I'm not going nuts, though, am I?"

"Never been saner, actually."

"That's something. Glad you turned up. It's been a pretty long trip...."

"Won't be much longer now."

"That little bastard managed to get me in the back. I was doing all right till then. Nothing much, of course. Just made me a bit slow. I was on my course for home, so I ought to be just about over the carrier. Radio's u/s, though. So I can't be sure."

"You're dead on your course, old boy. Easy as you go."

"Funny thing. I've gone numb. Must be the altitude or something. It's getting clearer down there. The sea looks—mortal empty, doesn't it? Maybe I'd better change course. Reckon I've missed her—"

"Keep straight on, Mike. Everything's fine."

"All right. If you're sure. Hell, I'm glad you came along. Don't mind telling you I'd got the breeze up quite a bit just now."

"Don't wonder. Felt the same way in my time. All right now?"

"Quite...all right. It's getting darker, though. Maybe that storm behind's catching us up. Can't hear the engine so well. There's nothing...wrong with that engine note, is there, Bill?"

"Not a thing, old boy. Just ease up a bit, that's all."

"It's getting...bloody dark. Can't see a thing. I say, Bill...."

"Yes, old boy?"

"Wasn't there something...something we used to say...something about darkness...."

"'Lighten our darkness'...?"

"That's it. Funny I should think of it suddenly. 'Lighten our darkness, we beseech thee, O Lord. And...and...'"

"'And in thy great mercy defend us from all perils and dangers....'"

"'Of this night.'"

"'Of...this...night....'" repeated Michael softly. He blinked as he looked at Bill. "Hullo, there you are. Sort of escort job, yours, isn't it?"

Bill grinned. "That sort of thing," he said.

They'd lit the bonfire on the green before it was really dark, so that as the last flames of the sunset were drained from the western sky they seemed to rise again in greater splendor from the twenty-foot pile of timber that the men and boys had been adding to all day. The bonfire was to have been ceremoniously touched off by the Mayor

Jane Oliver

after the King's speech had been relayed to the crowd which had attended the fancy dress parade in the Town Hall. But the strain of waiting had proved to be too much for various small boys. They had managed to get a box of matches from somewhere, and amused themselves for some time and with unexpected success by throwing them at the pile. So it happened that the emerging procession, headed by the Mayor and the Town Council, was greeted by the splendor of an unpremeditated conflagration, while the authors of it watched the official discomfiture from some distance up a tree.

Andrew had driven Mary and Verity down in the milk van after supper. Ted had rung up earlier in the day to say that his official duties would prevent him from getting home before the week end, but he would certainly be over then. He was cautious, though elated. "Doesn't do, of course, to let off too many guns. This isn't the end of everything. But it does bring the end nearer. Drink Michael's health in whatever you've got and start thinking of—well—say this time next year."

"We can only drink it in water," Mary said ruefully.

"Can't do that. It's unlucky."

"Don't be silly, darling," Mary said.

"Well—hrrmph—I'll see what I can do about it. Mind you all go out and enjoy yourselves tonight. Sure to be some sort of show on the green."

So they'd gone down to take part in the local celebrations, Mary and Andrew and Verity, and now they were standing by the bonfire listening to the choir which sometimes sang the songs they had practiced with the Vicar and the church organist, and sometimes the songs the crowd really wanted to hear. The flames from the skilfully laid bonfire tore at the overcast sky, turning it to an indigo backcloth against which the young green of the lime trees was patterned like a lattice of translucent jade. The branches themselves were often invisible, so that the dangling legs of the small boys who were clustered along them seemed almost miraculously suspended in mid-air. Below them, a great company of younger people were dancing round the bonfire, then pairing off to jig and trot in couples to the wheeze of an old accordion. They were wearing an odd assortment of clothes which had been concocted for a recent historical pageant in aid of the Red Cross and used again for the V Day fancy dress parade. So the scene had a strange, almost multidimensional aspect, as if the bonfire were not only celebrating the country's latest deliverance in 1945, but all those other occasions besides, on which her people had celebrated their escape from Danes or Frenchmen, the scattering of the Spanish Armada, or Nelson's victory at Trafalgar.

Behind the dancing masqueraders the older people stood more quietly, smiling at the antics of the youngsters, thinking of other youngsters elsewhere. The flames caught up the colors of the Allied flags that fluttered across cottage porches, were fastened along thatched roofs, stuck crookedly out of clipped yews in front gardens or from the

Jane Oliver

remains of last year's haystacks in the farmers' yards. They lit up the great red cross on its white ground that floated through the darkness over the church tower of St. Michael and All Angels, seventy feet above their heads. They lit up all the weathered or fresh faces of the people, touching into sudden pathos the smile of a middle-aged woman as she tucked her arm under her husband's, the careless beauty of a boy asking a girl to dance.

They lit up Mary's wondering face as she looked up at the big flag sailing through the air above them, remembering the day she had been married in that church, the day Michael had been christened there too. Michael... was he thinking of them too, that evening, thousands of inexorable miles away?

The choir was singing *Linden Lea* now, the dancers had thrown themselves down on the jewel-vivid turf to rest, and the accordion player was being offered a pint of beer. So only the naïve young voices rose against the roar and crackle of the flames. And Mary, looking round her, suddenly felt her own emotion reach out and blend again with that of the other women about her, some laughing, some in tears, some in the middle of their families, some quiet and alone. She was aware of other women, too, all over the country; in London, in industrial towns, in lonely places; in shepherds' cottages high in the Scottish hills, from which they could look down over the countryside and see fires springing up, fires that in the old days had meant danger, but now were beautiful on the mountains, publishing peace. Women in the liberated countries, where hope had blazed up again, after years of terror; women, too, in the countries that had been deceived and defeated, where hope itself must lie dead. So many women, smiling indulgently as they watched the thoughtless, noisy, exuberant celebrations of the young ones who hadn't had much excuse for gaiety in those long, hard years; other women, too, who could scarcely bear to look. Wasn't Tom or Jim or Harry out in Burma? Weren't so many boys still likely to go out East? Weren't their husbands, their sons, on the far side of death's awful engulfing silence, or almost as remote, it seemed, in the Japanese prison camps?

So Mary felt the tides of joy and grief, hope, anxiety, thankfulness and wild, uncalculating elation spin and flash and waver in the air about her almost as visibly as the sparks from the great bonfire that swirled up into the shadows above. She stood very still, letting them flow through her without resistance, tears brimming her wide-open eyes. It was then she heard him, heard for an instant Michael's voice come from the dimness beside Verity; his own, distinctive, gruff young voice, amused and confidential, using the very tones he used for her and her alone.

"*Think this beats the Jubilee bonfire, Mum? Seems pretty hot stuff to me....*"

("Oh, Michael, Michael, who had adored bonfires ever since he was a tiny boy!")

Mary felt as if an electric shock had gone through her. For a timeless instant of agony she could neither move nor speak. It did not occur to her to doubt that Michael was dead. The certainty had pierced too deeply towards the very core of her being, where the child himself had once lain. She had no words with which to express that knowledge; she was only sure, beyond all bodily questionings, of what her spirit knew. Scarcely knowing what she was doing she swung round on Verity, who still stood quietly beside her, panic blurring her voice as she said: "Verity—something—something's happened to Michael. I heard him speak to me—here—just now—"

Without a word Verity put her arms round her. Mary was shaking convulsively, and the hands with which she clutched at Verity struck cold. Verity neither questioned nor denied that knowledge; she just held Mary in her arms, till at last she stirred and moved away. Her face seemed to have changed, as if years had passed over her in those few minutes, leaving her stricken, quietened and wise.

"All right now?"

"Yes," Mary said. Then she went on slowly, as if she were trying to work things out. "He spoke to me. He sounded just like himself—whatever's happened to him. He was... fine. That's all I need to know... isn't it?"

"That's all you need," said Verity. "But it's hard... it's still hard... I wish—" She broke off, looking over Mary's shoulder. Andrew was still staring at the leaping fire, and something in his expression swept Verity with such a rush of pity that her eyes filled with the tears she had been unable to shed either for Michael or for herself. And Mary, watching her in astonishment, wondered why she'd never noticed before what a look of Michael Verity had. She said suddenly: "Verity, Andrew's going to be the one who'll need you most."

Verity said: "Yes, I know." And then she turned back to Mary, with all Michael's candor in her smile. "We're all going to need each other quite a bit," she said. Then, leaving Mary for a moment, she went over to Andrew and tugged at his coat till he turned, blinking.

"Let's... let's go home now, my dear," she said.

Things were quieter at the hospital now. Casualties were still coming in, but the rush had slackened. The out-patient departments were beginning to return to normal. Laura and Hugh were busy on a course of further training, Giles had been transferred to another area, Bill was still on liaison work with the Forces, and James at the lectures on the treatment of post-war neuroses which Mr. Prothero had refused to attend.

He shied away from the word neurosis; for he was now obsessed with the conviction that his own mind must be seriously deranged. How else could he account for the strangeness of his recent experiences, the inexplicable comings and goings, the occasional appearance of strange, celestial beings whom the credulous might have called angels, the stranger glimpses of hostile, darkened faces, ghastly among the chaos of a shaken world?

Jane Oliver 🦋

During the crisis of war everything but the work required of him had passed him by: he had been too busy to notice anything but the broken bodies of the patients under his hands. Like Laura, Hugh and James, he had worked under debris, in darkness, and among the flames of ruined cities. Sometimes he had caught glimpses of Giles in oilskins or Bill in flying kit. He had felt no surprise then at the strangeness of his changing environment, scarcely noticed his own increased mobility, been aware of neither weariness nor fear. The demands of the general emergency had swept him far beyond his habitual level of wary rationalism into a state of imaginative exaltation in which all things had been possible. But now, like Peter who had walked on the water without hesitation, he had begun to question the possibility of what he had actually done, and with the questioning had begun to sink.

Once more he was aware of himself, conscious of a loneliness which seemed the more appalling by contrast with the closeness of recent companionship. For, just as he came to realize his need for them, his friends seemed, unaccountably, to be no longer there. If a crisis in his personal life were approaching, it must, apparently, be encountered alone. The prospect caused him increasing anxiety. He began to worry about his family at the Cherry Orchard. How were things going for them? Was his wife's condition unchanged? Had anything else gone wrong?

MORNING FOR MR. PROTHERO

Mary was sitting on the seat at the far end of the rose alley, the fragments of a colored envelope at her feet, pleating and unpleating the oblong of a telegraph form with careful fingers.

"What's the matter?" said Mr. Prothero.

She turned towards him then. But she did not speak.

"Bad news?"

She nodded.

"Michael?"

"Yes."

"Wounded?"

"Missing on patrol. Believed—"

"No," said Mr. Prothero violently. "No—I won't believe it. Not Michael. Surely not Michael, of all people. It's too much—"

"Too much for any mother. Not just me—" said Mary. She sat very still, her shoulders bowed, as if not only by her own sorrow, but by so much more, by all the burdens borne by other mothers, up and down so many lands.

"I won't believe it," rebelled Mr. Prothero. "Mistakes are sometimes made. I've heard of them—"

"No."

"I'll make inquiries, have that news checked up. Don't believe the worst yet. If a mistake's been made I'll see someone suffers for it...." Mr. Prothero was aware of talking wildly, but he grappled with the situation as if even the thought of taking some action brought comfort. How were such inquiries made? He was out of touch. Who would know? James... Giles... Bill...? Yes, Bill, who worked with the Air Force. Bill would know.

He came on Bill outside the casualty receiving department. He was still in flying kit and looked as if he'd just come off patrol.

"Michael..." said Mr. Prothero abruptly. "Michael...?"

"He'll be all right when the shock wears off. They're fixing him up in there." Bill jerked his thumb towards the department he'd just left, then brought a heavy hand down on Mr. Prothero's shoulder. "Cheer up. What's wrong?"

"They've had news at his home. Missing, believed killed. It's not true then?"

"Oh yes, it's true all right," Bill said. "He's come across for good. But—" He broke off to stare at Mr. Prothero. "Surely you don't still think that death finishes anything? Not after all the work you've done here?"

Mr. Prothero shuddered convulsively, making a gesture of putting his hands over his ears. "I'm going mad..." he groaned. Then he flung back his head defiantly. "But while my wits last I refuse to be deluded by that sort of claptrap. Once the physical organism is shattered, what possibility of continued existence remains? Are you trying to tell me that Michael is dead?"

Brushing aside all regulations on the claim of extreme urgency, Bill answered bluntly:

"Yes, but so are you."

Mr. Prothero positively shook his fists at him. "Are you crazy, too?"

"Neither of us is, actually," said Bill, with a broad grin. "Look here, won't you consider the alternative? Supposing none of us were mad over here. Supposing you'd just got it wrong about the physical organism that you set so much store by? Didn't St. Paul give a broad enough hint when he spoke of a spiritual body? What else are you and I going about in? You and I've been what people across the Border call dead for the last twenty-five years."

"I won't believe it," said Mr. Prothero obstinately.

"Why not?" said Bill, stooping to ease the zip of one of his flying boots.

Why not? Mr. Prothero groped back among a lifetime's memories, aware in his bewilderment of another voice, a dry Scots voice which sounded in his ears above the clitter-clash of knitting needles. "I doubt we'll have to take ourselves back, Mr. Thomas, to the bit where we let a stitch go down."

Back then, back into the childhood he had almost forgotten, back to the shadows and splendors of the four-storied house in Regent's Park, to the point at which his serene infantile conception of an ordered earth and an improbable heaven in which God was surrounded by angels with six wings and saints who alternately threw down and retrieved their golden crowns, had been blasted like an oak by a lightning flash. Back to the moment when an angry, bewildered boy of thirteen found it impossible to reconcile the conventional piety of family prayers with the working conditions of his family's servants, remembering the disgraced little tweeny left sitting on her trunk outside the street door, the beating he had received for persistently helping a gasping housemaid to carry a scuttle of coal up four flights of stairs. Then and there he had identified God with his parents and flung his defiance at both. "If God's on your side... I'm on the other! I don't believe in God anyway." If God had existed, he remembered thinking, surely he would then have struck him dumb?

So now, while Bill swung his goggles on a finger tip and wondered, Mr. Prothero fought for the agnosticism of a lifetime with the same valor with which he had fought for mercy and truth, refusing hope as he had persistently refused all dulling anodynes. "If Michael's dead, it ends there. If I'm mad, they must shut me up. Don't try to take the edge off facts by quoting the Scriptures. I don't believe in God, I tell you...."

"Just as you like, Mr. Prothero," Bill said reasonably. "Well, I'd better move on, I suppose...."

Mr. Prothero was alone again. Obscurity closed in upon him as it once had done before, long ago. They'd said he was dying then. Were they right now? He panicked. If he could get out... breathe the fresh air... Desperately he plunged through the dimness... felt the smooth surface under his feet change to the roughness of turf... the softness of earth. He seemed to be wandering about a garden. Anywhere... it didn't matter. Michael was dead. He'd been fool enough to pray for him. Futile treachery. The whole thing was an illusion, as he'd always supposed. Back, then, back to the honest scepticism, back to the Stoic truth....

He blundered on, unutterably wretched, bereft both of his manhood's rationalism or the earlier beatific certainty of heaven which had been his birthright as a child. Tormented by the conflict within him, he tore his way forward, lurching through flowering shrubs, mowing down ranks of massed flowers. In the fog they seemed wraithlike, drained of color and life. Only here and there a few little flame-like blossoms shone through the obscurity like courage at the point of death.

Death... death... death! The word tolled in Mr. Prothero's mind like a knell. Michael was dead. There remained no hope, no vision, no possibility of prayer. His breath came in sobbing gasps. He stumbled and fell, struggled to his feet and fell again. This time he lay where he had fallen, beating with his fists on the ground, and jabbing his finger nails against the resistant turf, till at last his long pent bitterness escaped in tears.

Once he had lost control he could not regain it. He wept despairingly, as a child weeps, in the midst of an empty, echoing desolation that seemed infinite, and when the paroxysm died down at last he thought he must be light-headed. For in the obscurity he could hear voices, voices that were oddly backed by echoes, so that sometimes they seemed to come across a waste of centuries, and sometimes to be spoken close at hand in a language which was strange to him, so that how he knew their meaning he could not understand.

A voice that held the certainty of heaven said calmly:

"Why weepest thou?"

And the desolation of all bereaved humanity broke from the answering cry.

"Because they have taken away my Lord...and I know not where they have laid him...."

Mr. Prothero struggled to his feet and peered wildly through the mist. Before him stood the man he had supposed to be the gardener, and behind him a great stone was rolled away.

Helplessly, he stared, overcome less by the strangeness of what he was than by its familiarity, as if he had at last found the reality which had eluded him all his life long. He who had sought for truth, now saw it before him, he who had anguished with pity for all humanity, now saw pity itself for the first time; he who had loved those he sought to heal now saw love's living self face to face. But as the mist swirled back again he made his last, perversely heroic stand against the wishful thinking that he had fought all his life long. "I don't want hallucinations," said Mr. Prothero grimly. "Give me the truth."

From the far distance another voice, in its desperate honesty so like his own, came like an echo.

"Except I see in his hands the print of the nails...and put my finger into the print of the nails...I will not believe...."

"*Reach hither thy finger...*" said the man he had supposed to be the gardener. And as he spoke, the mist, too, began to roll away. About Mr. Prothero lay a vista which was no longer strange and splendid, but familiar as his own right hand. He had climbed every peak in the surrounding ring of summits, he knew every heuch and howe in the slopes of the wind-flattened bent that lay below him, tawny as the crust of a cottage loaf, the autumnal stretches of faded heather spreading across them like spilt wine. Here was no unknown country. He was standing in the doorway of Nanny's cottage, at the head of the Glaury Syke. About him were haystack and barn and twisted apple trees. Behind him the clitter-clash of knitting needles rose in a tiny stream of comforting sound, as Mr. Prothero instinctively sought their remembered reassurance. Round his neck he could fancy the clamping constriction of an Eton collar: against his knee the loving pressure of his uncomplaining dog. Glancing over his shoulder he saw Nanny herself, sitting in her rocking chair, knitting up what seemed to be the very sock he remembered seeing her take down. As the old chair creaked under the familiar heel-and-toe movement, he saw her nod and smile.

She did not speak, but in the distance Mr. Prothero thought he heard other voices. Laura was there, and James and Giles and Bill, Hugh and Joanna, Mary and Andrew (what was it Hugh had said...all part of the same creation, whichever side of the Border we're on?); Michael and Verity, hand in hand. But for Mr. Prothero a nearer voice seemed to catch up all their singing, and strange, triumphant words blazed like meteors across his mind.

"...*the Resurrection...and the Life*..."

Under their impact the prejudices of a lifetime cracked, crumbled and fell away like the prison walls of a chrysalis, leaving him free of his birthright of wonder as the newly born.

"Good...God!" whispered Thomas Prothero. He flung up a hand to shield his eyes. For all the splendors of his lost childhood's vision were singing and shining about him, and the long hidden sun had risen at last over the hills of home.

Across the centuries the awed voice of an earlier Thomas rolled towards him like an echo.

"*My Lord...and my God!*"

THIS EXCLUSIVE EDITION
*has been typeset for The Reincarnation Library
in Perpetua and Wade Sans and printed
by offset lithography on archival
quality paper
at Thomson-Shore, Inc.*

*The text and endpapers are acid-free and meet
or surpass all guidelines established by
the Council of Library Resources
and the American National
Standards Institute™.*

Book design by Charlotte Staub